discovering God's Word

discovering

God's Word

A 6-Week Introduction to the
Transformational Bible Study Method
with the GOSPEL of MARK

JEAN WILUND

Discovering God's Word: A 6-Week Introduction to the Transformational Bible Study Method with the Gospel of Mark
© 2025 by Jean S. Wilund

All rights reserved.

Requests for permission to quote from this book should be directed to: Permissions Department, Our Daily Bread Publishing, PO Box 3566, Grand Rapids, MI 49501; or contact us by email at permissionsdept@odbm.org.

Scripture quotations, unless otherwise indicated, are taken from the ESV® Bible (The Holy Bible, English Standard Version®), copyright © 2001 by Crossway, a publishing ministry of Good News Publishers. Used by permission. All rights reserved.

Scripture quotations marked BSB have been taken from the Holy Bible, Berean Standard Bible, BSB; 2016, 2020, 2023 by Bible Hub.

Interior design by Gayle Raymer and Michael J. Williams

ISBN: 978-1-64070-400-8

Library of Congress Cataloging-in-Publication Data Available

Printed in the United States of America

25 26 27 28 29 30 31 32 / 8 7 6 5 4 3 2 1

To my children and grandchildren—to a thousand generations
—Bobby, Kaitlyn, Ophelia, Samuel, Brittany, and Carolyn:

I wrote this study for you.
I pray the Lord will use it to bless others, but I wrote it for you.
My heart beats with yours every day.
My thoughts are consumed with prayers for you.
My love for you reaches as high as the highest heavens.

If God allowed me only one prayer for you, I'd pray that you would know, love, and believe the Lord your God and His Word with all your heart, soul, mind, and strength.
Forever.

Heaven and earth will pass away, but my words will not pass away.
—Mark 13:31

Contents

Start Here 9
God's Purpose, Call, and Promise for Bible Study 11

WEEK ONE
A Firm Foundation (MARK 1:1–45) 13

WEEK TWO
A Heart to Receive (MARK 2:1–5:43) 45

WEEK THREE
Eyes to See (MARK 6:1–8:38) 81

WEEK FOUR
Ears to Hear (MARK 9:1–10:52) 119

WEEK FIVE
Behold Your King! (MARK 11:1–13:37) 153

WEEK SIX
Follow Your King (MARK 14:1–16:8) 189

Attributes of God 221
Notes 223
Resources 225
Thank You! 227

Start Here

To best prepare you for this study, I offer one spiritual truth and four recommendations.

ONE SPIRITUAL TRUTH: THE BIBLE IS A SPIRITUAL BOOK

God is the author of His divine Word. To understand the Bible, we need God's Spirit. "For who knows a person's thoughts except the spirit of that person, which is in him? So also no one comprehends the thoughts of God except the Spirit of God" (1 Corinthians 2:11).

If you've trusted in Christ for your salvation, you've received His Spirit to guard and keep you and to help you understand His Word.

"Now we have received not the spirit of the world, but the Spirit who is from God, that we might understand the things freely given us by God. And we impart this in words not taught by human wisdom but taught by the Spirit, interpreting spiritual truths to those who are spiritual" (1 Corinthians 2:12–13).

Anyone who doesn't belong to Christ will struggle to study the Bible effectively. "The natural person does not accept the things of the Spirit of God, for they are folly to him, and he is not able to understand them because they are spiritually discerned" (1 Corinthians 2:14).

If you're not a Christian, the gospel of Mark reveals the way to salvation in Christ. If you want to talk with someone about how to receive salvation, reach out to me at JeanWilund.com or the people at Our Daily Bread Ministries at odbm.org/about-us/contact-us.

FOUR RECOMMENDATIONS

1. Read all of the gospel of Mark.

Reading straight through a book of the Bible before we slow down to study it can help us grasp the overall picture and zero in on the author's main message—the heartbeat of his book that reverberates through the chapters. As you read, strap on a proverbial pair of ancient sandals and step into the setting. Be present with all five senses. Read Mark in a day or two—or over several days. It's a fast-paced read, but there are sixteen chapters. You'll have two days at the beginning of Week One to read all of Mark, but I recommend you get an early start.

2. Understand what this study is and isn't.

Discovering God's Word is two studies in one—a study on how to study the Bible and a study on the gospel of Mark. Because we're examining how to study the Bible, we don't have time to dive deep into every aspect of Mark, but you'll walk away with a firm grasp on the book—and transformed by Mark's message.

3. Discover more Bible study resources at JeanWilund.com.

To enhance this study (and your study of every book of the Bible), I offer additional resources and helps on the *Discovering God's Word* page on my website.

4. Study with a group.

Studying with a group can provide additional accountability and encouragement (Ephesians 4:11–16). You'll find helpful discussion questions and podcast episodes on the *Discovering God's Word* page on my website, JeanWilund.com.

God's Purpose, Call, and Promise for Bible Study

> Your words were found, and I ate them, and your words became to me a joy and the delight of my heart, for I am called by your name, O Lord, God of hosts.
> —Jeremiah 15:16

The Bible is God's divine revelation—the unveiling of who He is, His divine will, and His salvation through Jesus Christ.

God's purpose for Bible study isn't to make us better people—better Christians. Instead, His purpose is to glorify Himself through Christ and His gospel as we come to know Him. "For from him and through him and to him are all things. To him be glory forever. Amen" (Romans 11:36).

God's call is for people everywhere to read His Word to know Him and His salvation (2 Timothy 3:14–17) and to obey Him out of a natural overflow of love for Him (John 14:15). "This is eternal life, that they know you, the only true God, and Jesus Christ whom you have sent" (John 17:3).

God's promise for those who belong to Him is transformation as we study and walk in obedience to His Word. "I am sure of this, that he who began a good work in you will bring it to completion at the day of Jesus Christ" (Philippians 1:6).

I pray that over the next six weeks, God will glorify Himself through you as His Word transforms you and makes you more like Christ—and fills you with His abiding peace and joy.

WEEK ONE

A Firm Foundation

MARK 1:1–45

His divine power has granted to us all things that pertain to life and godliness, through the knowledge of him who called us to his own glory and excellence.

—2 Peter 1:3

WEEK ONE — day one

Overview

TODAY'S READING

Read the gospel of Mark over the next few days.

Imagine the thunder of the ocean's waves, the majesty of snow-clad mountains, and the coolness of soft grass under your bare feet. God's soul-stirring creation declares His glory—the glory of their creator. Along with the heavens, they shout His praise from the rising of the sun to its setting (Psalms 19:1; 113:3).

But how do we know where the majesty we see came from?

We know from God's Word. Apart from the Bible, we're left to discern on our own—or through the imaginations of others—the source of creation and the character, nature, and ways of the Creator.

To truly know anything about God, we need His written Word.

> We'll never truly know the God of the Word apart from the Word of God.

To understand God's written Word, we need His Spirit and an understanding of effective Bible study. Earthly minds can never understand the thoughts and ways of the Infinite without all three—God's Spirit, His Word, and an effective way to study it.

We'll use the gospel of Mark to train ourselves to study His Word well while God uses Mark to transform us—if we truly believe and obey what He says.

THE TRANSFORMATIONAL BIBLE STUDY METHOD

Before we dive into the details of effective Bible study, let's look at an overview of the three simple steps that form the basis of our study method.

STEP ONE: INTENT

*What did God intend His original
audience to understand?*

The first question in the Transformational Bible Study Method focuses on what God, the true Author, intended the original recipients of His message to understand. Each human author God chose to relay His message wrote directly to an ancient audience, but they also wrote for the benefit of every believer in every generation.

> Knowing this first of all, that no prophecy of Scripture comes from someone's own interpretation. For no prophecy was ever produced by the will of man, but men spoke from God as they were carried along by the Holy Spirit. (2 Peter 1:20–21)

STEP TWO: TRUTH

*What truths does God's Word reveal about the
character, nature, and ways of our triune God,
and that of anyone or anything other than Him?*

When we see the Lord as He truly is, we can then—and only then—rightly view everyone and everything else, including ourselves and our circumstances. This is why the second question focuses us first on discovering the eternal truths about our triune God's character, nature, and ways as He's revealed Himself in Scripture. We also want to learn the character, nature, and ways of sin, Satan, his dominion of darkness, the world, and our human nature—who we are *without* Christ (Romans 8:5–7) and who we are *in* Christ (Romans 8:9–17).

> His divine power has granted to us all things that pertain to life and godliness, through the knowledge of him who called us to his own glory and excellence. (2 Peter 1:3)

STEP THREE: TRANSFORMATION

> *If I truly believe and act on what God has revealed in His Word, how will the desires and attitudes of my heart transform and my actions be different tomorrow?*

God didn't give us the Bible to stuff our heads with knowledge but to transform us into the image of Christ (Romans 8:29; 2 Corinthians 3:18). Our goal isn't to learn how to conquer the Bible but to let the Bible conquer us—to make God's will our will (Philippians 2:12–13). Through this final question, we reflect on the truths revealed through Scripture and ask ourselves what it looks like to rightly respond to them. A biblical response naturally overflows out of belief and into obedience to God's Word, which ultimately leads to authentic and lasting transformation—to loving the Lord with all our heart, soul, mind, and strength.

> Jesus answered him, "If anyone loves me, he will keep my word." (John 14:23)

HOW DO I RESPOND?

The heavens declare the glory of God, and our lives will, too, when we realize that spiritual transformation isn't a work of our efforts but a work of faith in the Father, Son, and Holy Spirit.

> The heavens declare the glory of God,
>   and the sky above proclaims his handiwork.
>   (Psalm 19:1)

We see God's handiwork on every page of Scripture. The Bible reveals aspects of God's glorious character, nature, and ways on every page—attributes such as

- God is our majestic Creator.
- Jesus Christ is our unfailing Savior.
- The Holy Spirit is our empowering Teacher and Guide.

TRANSFORMATIONAL TRUTH

We'll never truly know the God of the Word apart from the Word of God.

In the "Attributes of God" section at the back of this book or in a separate journal, begin a list of God's attributes (His character, nature, and ways) and add to it continually. Note one or two attributes of God you noticed in the gospel of Mark today.

I mentioned that obedience overflows from belief. If you truly believe in the importance of studying God's Word, what will this look like in your life? How will you respond? If you struggle to find time, ask God to show you where you can make time in your day to abide in His Word. As the Creator of time, He'll help you set aside time. Journal your response.

_____

_____

_____

_____

_____

_____

_____

_____

_____

_____

_____

_____

TRANSFORMATIONAL BIBLE STUDY PRINCIPLES

- ✓ Knowing the Bible author's *intent* helps us better interpret God's authoritative *truth*, which leads to authentic *transformation* for all who belong to Christ and believe His Word.
- ✓ Keep the *Intent*, *Truth*, and *Transformation* questions in mind whenever you study the Bible.

MEMORY VERSE

Memorizing God's Word allows Scripture to linger in our minds and sink deeper into our hearts. Write out this week's memory verse and read it aloud five times.

His divine power has granted to us all things that pertain to life and godliness, through the knowledge of him who called us to his own glory and excellence. (2 Peter 1:3)

WEEK ONE — *day two*

Step One: Intent

TODAY'S READING

Continue to read through Mark.

I found a letter in my parents' attic written to my dad. The letter was dated April 13, 1974. The author of the letter begged him for a two-week old kitten. No one signed the letter, but telltale signs give the author away.

GOD'S INTENT

The Bible is a letter of much greater importance than the desire for a kitten. It's a letter from God written *for* us and our salvation, but not written directly *to* us. We weren't the original audience. But from the beginning, God intended their words to benefit us as well.

INTENT QUESTION
What did God intend His original audience to understand?

> Now these things happened **to them** as an example,
> but they were written down **for our** instruction,
> on whom the end of the ages has come.
> (1 Corinthians 10:11)

More than forty human authors wrote, as the Holy Spirit directed them, to the people of their day. As we study the Bible, our goal is to discern each verse's meaning as originally intended.

To help us discover a passage's meaning, we'll consider its context as well as the genre, writing styles, and writing techniques the author used. We'll examine these factors later, but first let's ground ourselves in basic introductory information. We want to learn about the human author, his audience, and the main purpose God gave him for writing.

In today's lesson, we'll gather introductory information for the gospel of Mark.

PRACTICE SESSION: INTRODUCTION TO MARK

To find introductory information, I suggest three search methods.

1. Search the book of the Bible we're studying.

Some authors (such as the prophets and most writers of the Epistles) identified themselves and offered some background information. Mark didn't. The author never signed his name, dated his book, or identified his audience. We can, however, discern his purpose for writing.

- **Read Mark 1:1–3 and Mark 16:6–8 and look for hints at the heartbeat of Mark's gospel.** Some authors allude to their central message at the beginning and end of their book. From these verses, consider what theme or main message Mark might want his audience to understand, and summarize it below. We'll confirm and/or refine our understanding as we study.

_____

_____

_____

_____

2. Search the rest of the Bible.

The Bible is one connected story. A question in one book is often answered in another. The more we read and study the whole Bible, the easier it gets to see its pieces fitting together. Over time, we begin to see more and more connections.

3. Search biblical resources.

Study Bibles and Bible handbooks typically offer book introductions. Some websites offer free book introductions. Let's go to one of these resources now.

Start by going to my website, JeanWilund.com, and clicking on Helpful Resources. (I update these resources to ensure they remain current.) Click on Book Introductions, then click on a link to a resource site. Once there, find and select Mark. Use one or more of the introductions to Mark to answer the following questions.

Author: Who wrote Mark? _____

Date: When was Mark written? _____

Audience: Who was Mark's audience? _____

Purpose: What is Mark's central message? _____

_____

MEET MARK

The author of Mark's gospel didn't sign his book, but he left telltale signs of his authorship, freeing us to confidently call it the gospel of Mark rather than the gospel of We Don't Know. First-century church leaders unanimously attributed this gospel to Mark. They knew him. The early church met in his mother's home (Acts 12:12).

Mark wasn't one of the twelve disciples, but it's believed he witnessed Christ's ministry and served as the apostle Peter's assistant in Rome. He first served as a missionary assistant to Paul and Barnabas—but then deserted them (Acts 15:37–40). Through the power of the Holy Spirit and the devoted discipleship of Peter, God transformed Mark into a faithful servant of Christ (2 Timothy 4:11; 1 Peter 5:13).

Mark wrote to gentile Christians in Rome to encourage this persecuted church to pick up their cross and follow their king, Jesus Christ. Jesus is the Son of God and Son of Man, who came not to be served but to serve, suffer for their salvation (and ours), and defeat Satan and his dominion of darkness.

HOW DO I RESPOND?

Of all the men God could have chosen to write this gospel account, He chose Mark, a man who'd failed to be faithful—like Peter, the man who discipled him. Simon Peter denied Christ three times. Christ transformed both Peter and Mark from failure to faithful by the power of the Holy Spirit and the truth of His Word.

Do you ever feel frustrated in your faithfulness to Christ or to Bible study?

Do you struggle to live out what you say you believe?

Whatever your struggle, let Mark's (and Peter's) story encourage you. Christ restores, equips, and empowers His children. It's never too late to be transformed.

Now that we've solved the mystery of the gospel of Mark's author, let's solve the mystery of my 1974 kitten letter. The telltale signs point to me as the author. I recognize my handwriting at age nine. Sadly, I failed to accomplish my will. I didn't get the kitten. Mark's letter, however, continues to accomplish God's will—as does all of God's Word. "He who calls you is faithful; he will surely do it" (1 Thessalonians 5:24).

- List your biggest struggles in studying the Bible. Is it time? Desire? Lack of faithfulness to follow through? Pray and ask God to help you overcome these struggles.

_____

_____

_____

_____

_____

TRANSFORMATIONAL TRUTH

It's never too late to be transformed. Christ restores, equips, and empowers His children.

Add to your Attributes of God list at the back of the book.

If you truly believe and act on what God has revealed in today's passage, what will it look like? What habits will you create (or change) as you study the Bible? How might obedience to God's calling lead you to trust Him to restore, equip, or empower you to faithfully follow Him? Journal your response.

_____
_____
_____
_____
_____
_____
_____
_____
_____
_____

TRANSFORMATIONAL BIBLE STUDY PRINCIPLES

- ✓ The Bible was written *for* us, not *to* us.
- ✓ The Bible is one connected story. A question in one book is often answered in another.
- ✓ Study Bibles and Bible handbooks offer book introductions that summarize each Bible book's author, audience, date, and purpose for his message.

MEMORY VERSE: 2 PETER 1:3

Write out this week's memory verse.

WEEK ONE — *day three*

Step Two: Truth (Part 1)

TODAY'S READING

Mark 1:1–11

In *The Knowledge of the Holy*, A. W. Tozer writes, "What comes to mind when we think about God is the most important thing about us."

I couldn't say it better.

TRUTH QUESTION

What truths does God's Word reveal about the character, nature, and ways of God the Father, Son, and Holy Spirit?

THE TRUTH ABOUT GOD

What we think about God determines what we think about everything else. He's our starting point for viewing everything in life. The better we know Him, the less deceived we are about everything else. He reveals truths about Himself on every page of the Bible. As we study it, questions like the following help uncover what we need to know about God:

- Do we see the Father, Son, or Holy Spirit at work in this passage? If so, what truths or attributes does their work reveal?
- What, if any, aspects of the gospel or Christ's coming kingdom does the passage display?
- Are any names or titles of the Father, Son, or Holy Spirit mentioned in the passage? If so, what do they teach us?

TRUTH CHART (T-CHART)

The first time I read through the Bible, I began to list on paper truths I saw in Scripture about God. Soon after, I drew a line down the middle of the paper and began to list on the right side any key truths I noticed in Scripture about everything and everyone else.

With lists of truths on both sides of the paper, I could compare and contrast God with everyone and everything else—and I had discovered the power of the T-chart. These comparisons and contrasts helped me understand God (and everyone else) more clearly, which led to my being better able to faithfully interpret and respond to Scripture.

Bullet point key information and truths into columns under keyword headings that reflects the main "character(s)" in the passage. Look for connections and spiritual truths to pop off the page. In the sample T-chart below, I've listed helpful tips.

TRIUNE GOD	OTHERS
IDENTIFY: **FATHER, SON, AND/ OR HOLY SPIRIT**	*FOR EXAMPLE:* **PHARISEES/SCRIBES**
• On the left side of the chart, I note truths or key information the passage contains about God the Father, Son, and/or the Holy Spirit. • If a verse or passage doesn't mention God, I leave it blank. We never want to force information into the text.	• On the right side of the chart, I note truths or key information the passage contains about anyone and/or anything else other than God. • If I wonder about a point, I note my question and find the answer later, either in Scripture or in a commentary. • If a verse or passage only mentions God and not *others*, I leave this side blank. We never want to force information into the text. • The fewer the words, the better.

The T-chart is a simple tool to help us better see connections and truths as we study. Being a visual processor, I often use different colored pens or highlighters to draw arrows and circles as I compare and contrast the information. My charts are a jumble of scribbled notes, but they help me better interpret the Scriptures. Keep it simple, and don't chain yourself to the chart, but don't underestimate its helpfulness either. (See my website for printed blank templates: JeanWilund.com.)

PRACTICE SESSION: MARK 1:1–11

INTENT

- Heralds in ancient Rome announced the arrival of their king at the city gates.
- John's clothing and ministry resembled that of Old Testament prophets.
- The Old Testament prophets Isaiah and Malachi prophesied John the Baptist's ministry (Isaiah 40:3–5; Malachi 3:1; 4:5).

TRUTH

Read Mark 1:1–11. As you read, step into the wilderness. Imagine Mark as an ancient Roman herald proclaiming Christ's long-awaited arrival. "Hear ye! Hear ye! It has begun! What all creation has longed to see since the serpent's temptation in the garden has begun—the beginning of the gospel of Jesus Christ, the Son of God."

Imagine Isaiah's voice speaking from the past. Stand at the edge of the Jordan as John baptizes Jesus. Watch the Holy Spirit descend and listen to the voice of the Father from above.

On the left side of your T-chart, note what Mark reveals about our triune God. (We'll talk about the right side, "Others," tomorrow.)

I'll start. You add.

TRIUNE GOD	OTHERS
FATHER • God[1] = *theos* (Greek) = the Supreme Divinity • Fulfilled Scripture by sending John the Baptist to prepare for Jesus • Initiates salvation • Keeps His promises	
JESUS (SON) • Jesus[2] = *iēsous* (Greek) = Joshua = "Yahweh is salvation" • *Yahweh* is God's relational, promise-keeping name • Christ[3] = *christos* (Greek) = *Messiah* (Hebrew) "anointed" or "set apart" • God set Jesus apart to save us	
HOLY SPIRIT	

You'll see I used a concordance to look up the original meaning of names and titles for Jesus. To access a free *Strong's Concordance*, visit the Helpful Resources page at JeanWilund.com for links to websites that offer free concordances.

TRANSFORMATION

What comes to your mind when you think about God?

Many Christians have too few thoughts about Him—or wrong ones—because they've lost (or never understood) the importance of reading and studying the Bible. May we determine to read and study God's Word every day and proclaim God's glory and gospel to the world like Mark. "Hear ye! Hear ye! The gospel of Jesus Christ!"

TRANSFORMATIONAL TRUTH

What we think about God determines what we think about everything else.

Add to your Attributes of God list at the back of the book.

In true herald fashion, write a proclamation about our triune God. Include truths Mark reveals about God in today's passage and consider what it will look like in your life if you truly believe these truths.

Hear ye! Hear ye! . . .

DAY THREE | 31

_____
_____
_____
_____
_____
_____
_____

TRANSFORMATIONAL BIBLE STUDY PRINCIPLES

- ✓ Truth Question, Part 1: What truths does God's Word reveal about the character, nature, and ways of God the Father, Son, and Holy Spirit?
- ✓ As you study, create T-charts of truths God's Word reveals about the Father, Son, and Holy Spirit.

MEMORY VERSE: 2 PETER 1:3

Write out this week's memory verse.

WEEK ONE — *day four*

Step Two: Truth (Part 2)

TODAY'S READING

Mark 1:12–15

You will be like God.

These deceitful words slithered from Satan's tongue and enticed Eve to embrace a wretched lie about herself: I can be like God. I can decide for myself what is good and right.

THE TRUTH ABOUT OTHERS

Since that inglorious day, when sin enticed and deceived Adam and Eve, sin has been working its evil in us, enticing us to embrace countless lies about ourselves, the world, sin, Satan, and salvation (Romans 5:12). But God gave us a glorious solution. "You will know the truth, and the truth will set you free" (John 8:32).

> **TRUTH QUESTION**
>
> *What truths does God's Word reveal about the character, nature, and ways of anyone or anything other than God?*

All truth leads us to the One who is the Truth—Jesus Christ. God transforms even the vilest of the vile who know and trust in the Truth. As fallen creatures, however, we're prone to trust the world's philosophies, our own foolish wisdom, and even Satan's lies more than Christ unless we truly know and believe what God has said about Himself and others. Jesus warns us to be on our guard against sin and its traps, Satan and his schemes, the world and its enticements, and our own hearts both *before* and *after* we belong to Christ (Matthew 10:16). Questions like the following help us uncover scriptural truths that can keep us free from sin's grip.

- What does the passage we've read reveal about the character, nature, or ways of sin, Satan, and/or the dominion of darkness? Do we see Satan, demons, or any power of darkness at work in this passage? If so, what are they doing and what does this teach us?
- Do we see any character traits of what we're like either before or after we've trusted in Christ?
- What does the author want us to understand about ourselves?
- How does the setting, plot, characters, or objects in the passage reveal important truths?

Yesterday we looked for what Mark reveals about our triune God. Today we're only looking for what Mark reveals about anyone *other* than God.

PRACTICE SESSION: MARK 1:12–15

INTENT

- The Bible often uses the number forty to represent trials, suffering, and testing (Deuteronomy 8:2).
- The *wilderness* is often used in the Bible as a place of testing and trials designed to reveal the faithfulness of God and the faith of those being tested (Exodus 15–40).
- Angels are spiritual beings created by God to serve Him and His children (Hebrews 1:5–14).

TRUTH

Pray and read Mark 1:12–15. Step into this passage and walk into the wilderness with Jesus but watch for wild animals. Imagine being tempted by Satan for forty days. Make notes in the T-chart as you answer the second part of the Truth question. I'll start.

TRIUNE GOD	OTHERS
	SATAN
	• Relentlessly tempted Jesus for 40 days
	ANGELS
	JOHN THE BAPTIST

- If Satan would relentlessly pursue Jesus for forty days to entice Him to sin, what should we humans expect from Satan?
- Consider why Mark mentioned wild animals—as in ravaging wolves, not fluffy bunnies.
- Read Genesis 3:1, the introduction to Adam and Eve's fall to temptation.
- What do we learn through John the Baptist about discipleship and its cost? (See John 3:30.)

Satan is merciless, relentless, and a clever liar. He's also defeated. Jesus was never at Satan's mercy. Neither was John—even in prison. Satan is like a dog on a leash, only able to go as far as his Master allows. He can only do what God permits, and God only permits what He'll work for our good and His glory—as He did with Jesus in the wilderness for forty days.

Jesus is our victorious and sinless Savior, loved and cared for by His Father.

John was God's faithful servant. He fulfilled the work God gave him to do.

The time had come for Jesus's ministry to increase and John's to decrease (John 3:30)—and for John to receive his great and eternal rewards in heaven.

TRANSFORMATION

Whether we realize it or not, our sinful hearts echo Adam's and Eve's when they embraced Satan's lie—that we can be like God. Scripture reveals every truth we need to know to stand against sin's allure and Satan's schemes. We need to know the truth about Satan's lies so it's as futile for Satan to tempt Christians to doubt God's character and word as it was futile for Satan to tempt Jesus.

When we know God's Word, the truth guards our hearts and minds from the inflated lies of Satan, the world, and our own hearts. Just as the truth brought Christ through Satan's temptations in the wilderness, the truth will bring us through our trials.

When (not *if*) you face unjust trials, remember God has a good purpose for it. Don't despair. Remember the truth.

When (not *if*) you're tempted, silence sin and Satan's lies by speaking the truth to your heart—and believing the truth.

When (not *if*) your heart deceives you about the truth, the lies will sink their fangs into you—but the truth will set you free. Learn, remember, and believe the truth.

TRANSFORMATIONAL TRUTH

Trials reveal the truth about our faith and God's faithfulness.

Add to your Attributes of God list at the back of the book.

If you truly believe the truths God's Word reveals about sin, Satan, the world, and us in today's passage, what will it look like in your life? How will you respond like Christ in your trials and suffering? Journal your response.

TRANSFORMATIONAL BIBLE STUDY PRINCIPLES

- ✓ Truth Question, Part 2: What truths does God's Word reveal about the character, nature, and ways of anyone or anything other than God?
- ✓ Do we see any character traits of what we're like either before or after we've trusted in Christ?
- ✓ What does the author want us to understand about ourselves?
- ✓ How does the setting, plot, characters, or objects in the passage reveal important truths?

MEMORY VERSE: 2 PETER 1:3

Write out this week's memory verse.

WEEK ONE — *day five*

Step Three: Transformation

TODAY'S READING

Mark 1:16–45

If you wanted to form a team of men to establish the most important institution in history, would you wander among thieves, political rebels, and fishing boats to find your leaders? Would you choose men who would deny and abandon you in your most anguished hour?

Jesus did.

AUTHENTIC TRANSFORMATION

God's Word always does God's work in God's people. His greatest work (and our greatest need) is spiritual salvation that changes us from *sinner* to *saint*, *enemy of God* to *child of God*, and *condemned* to *redeemed*. Christ and His salvation are the main point of the Bible and our sole means of salvation.

Once God saves us, He begins His next great work—our transformation, aka *sanctification*. Sanctification is God's process of transforming us to make us more like His Son (Romans 8:29). He uses His Word to teach us; His Spirit to convict, encourage, and empower us; and our

> **TRANSFORMATION QUESTION**
>
> *If I truly believe and act on what God has revealed in this passage, how will the desires and attitudes of my heart transform, and how will my actions be different tomorrow? What does it look like to believe and obey?*

circumstances to give us endless opportunities for our faith to reveal what we truly believe.

What we *truly* believe spills out into our action, whether our beliefs are based on the truth or a lie. The ER receives a fair share of patients whose actions flow out of beliefs grounded in error. The gun isn't loaded. Drugs aren't that bad. I can make that jump. We need to ground ourselves in the truth of God's Word—and believe it. We can say we believe God's Word, but do our lives prove we actually believe otherwise?

Over our lifetime our sin-saturated human nature has developed habits that oppose the truth and induce destructive pride and/or anxiety. Knowing the Bible isn't the only key. Knowing and believing it is. No matter how much we master the Bible, until the Bible masters us, we'll remain unchanged—and likely grow insufferable through pride over our vast knowledge.

This conundrum is why the Transformation Question is so valuable. Rather than ask what we need to *do* with what we've read in God's Word, which can develop a "works-based" faith, we ask what our actions will look like if we truly believe the truths.

WILL, NOT *CAN*

Transformation isn't about what we *can* do, but what we *will* do *if* we truly believe (James 2:14–26). It's not enough to verbally agree with Christ that we *can* obey His Word. If we truly believe, we will obey. Obedience is the natural overflow of belief.

Our actions reveal what we believe. Either we'll change what we believe to agree with our actions, or we'll change our actions to align with our beliefs. Fortunately, Christ's authority and sufficiency exceed even the most impossible situations. No one is too tough for God to transform—not you, your loved ones, or those in today's passage.

PRACTICE SESSION: MARK 1:16–45

INTENT

- In Jesus's day, the disciples (and the world) were only just discovering the truth about Christ's authority and sufficiency to transform lives. In the case of the religious leaders, they disputed His authority. They couldn't dispute His sufficiency.

TRUTH

Read Mark 1:16–45. I didn't include a Truth chart today because we're focused on the Transformation question—but remember, the truth transforms, so always look for the truths God reveals in His Word.

In each passage below, list the outward evidence of any physical and/or spiritual transformation. Over what power or people did Jesus reveal His sufficiency and authority to transform, and what does their transformation teach us about Christ?

I'll start.

Mark 1:16–20

- **Transformation:** Simon, Andrew, James, and John left everything and followed Jesus when He called them.
- **Truth about Jesus:** Jesus transforms hearts. When He calls, His sheep follow (John 10:3–4).

Mark 1:21–28

- **Transformation:** _____

- **Truth about Jesus:** _____

Mark 1:29–38

- **Transformation:** _____

- **Truth about Jesus:** _____

Mark 1:39–45

- **Transformation:** _____

  _____

- **Truth about Jesus:** _____

  _____

In the midst of Christ's miracles and preaching, what indispensable aspect of Jesus's ministry and power did Mark record in Mark 1:35?

_____

How will you approach prayer if you truly believe it's as important as Jesus's life demonstrated?

_____

_____

_____

TRANSFORMATION

When Jesus chose the men He wanted to establish and build His church, He chose common fishermen, a political zealot, and a hated tax collector. They weren't men we'd have chosen. I wonder if part of the reason He selected this unimpressive lot is so their transformation would bring Him more glory. Just as Christ worked in His disciples, He works in us. He saves us and makes us His sons and daughters and co-heirs with Christ, all in a moment (Romans 8:17). He transforms us into the image of Christ in time (Romans 8:29). Some of us take more time than others, but don't despair. We may fall onto our face rather than our faith, but Christ will restore and transform us in and by the truth.

TRANSFORMATIONAL TRUTH

God's Word always does God's work in God's people.

Add to your Attributes of God list at the back of the book.

What will it look like in your life if you truly believe God's Word rather than what the world says, what your fears whisper, or what your pride demands? How will you respond when trials come or when you don't get your way? How will your fears be quieted when God doesn't answer your prayers yet—or like you hoped? Journal your response.

TRANSFORMATIONAL BIBLE STUDY PRINCIPLES

- ✓ Transformation Question: If I truly believe and act on what God has revealed in this passage, how will the desires and attitudes of my heart transform and my actions be different tomorrow? What does it look like to believe and obey?
- ✓ Transformation isn't about what we *can* do, but what we *will* do *if* we truly believe.
- ✓ No matter how much we master the Bible, until the Bible masters us, we'll remain unchanged.

MEMORY VERSE: 2 PETER 1:3

Write out this week's memory verse.

WEEK TWO

A Heart to *Receive*

MARK 2:1–5:43

Do your best to present yourself to God as one approved, a worker who has no need to be ashamed, rightly handling the word of truth.
—2 Timothy 2:15

WEEK TWO — day one

Assumptions

TODAY'S READING
Mark 2:1–3:6

Assumptions can lead to trouble.

Consider the toddler wobbling toward his preschool's jungle gym. Just as he is about to ram his head on a metal bar, his teacher hollers, "Duck!" The little boy quacks at his teacher—and whacks his head.

THE TROUBLE WITH ASSUMPTIONS

The job—and privilege—of every Christian is to properly interpret the Bible so we don't assume the authors meant "imitate a waterfowl" when they actually meant "watch your head."

Assumptions are thoughts or ideas we believe to be true without putting much, if any, thought to them. Multiple factors shape our assumptions, such as our background, experiences, personality, age, language, education, culture, and beliefs (whether right or wrong). As we study to know the truth, we discover the truth about our assumptions—whether they were right or wrong.

For example, before I trusted in Christ and studied the Bible, I wrongly assumed the Bible was a book written by men for men to record their thoughts about God. After I became a Christian and studied the Bible, I discovered the Bible is the very words of God directed by His Spirit to His chosen authors. I also discovered that there is ample evidence—both archaeological and historical—that the Bible is true. Whenever I read the Bible now, I know—rather than assume—every word is trustworthy and true.

If we're not careful, we'll make wrong assumptions about the Bible. It's an ancient book written to a vastly different audience who spoke a language we don't understand, and it concerns deep spiritual truths. Whenever we don't understand what the Bible says, let's carefully examine—not cross-examine—the text to discover its true meaning.

EXAMINE—NOT CROSS-EXAMINE—SCRIPTURE

When we *examine* God's Word, we put it under a microscope of Holy Spirit–dependent prayer, clarifying questions, and careful observation so we can better understand what God wants us to know and believe through the passage.

When we *cross-examine* God's Word, we put it on trial and demand it answer to us and our beliefs, opinions, and assumptions.

Examining God's Word comes from a place of humility; cross-examining it rises from pride.

The religious leaders questioned Jesus out of their prideful hearts. They cross-examined Him to indict Him (Luke 11:53). One particular Pharisee, however, questioned Jesus with sincere motives. Nicodemus wanted to understand, not challenge, Jesus's difficult teaching (John 3:1–21).

Since we can't avoid forming assumptions, let's resolve to move beyond them to the truth through prayer, sincere clarifying questions, and observation. The more, the better. We may have tired our mothers with our persistent questions, but we won't tire God. Before we ask, though, let's make sure we're truly willing to hear and learn the truth.

The truth sets us free. Anything else destroys.

THREE TIPS FOR ASKING GOOD CLARIFYING QUESTIONS

1. Look at the questions our all-knowing God and Christ ask. Since they never need information, their questions always lead to the truth, including exposing the truth of someone's lie.
2. Pay attention to the questions others ask. You may have the same questions.
3. Ask *who, what, when, why, how,* or *did* over and over until there's no more who, what, when, why, how, or did left to ask.

In today's lesson, we'll recognize the influence of assumptions and the value of clarifying questions.

PRACTICE SESSION: MARK 2:1–3:6

Pray and read Mark 2:1–3:6. Consider any assumptions you might bring to the text or form as you read. Use the three tips above to list as many clarifying questions as you can that could help lead you to the truth. I'll start with Mark 2:1–7.

MY ASSUMPTIONS	MY CLARIFYING QUESTIONS
• Jesus was preaching the gospel. • All four men and the paralytic must have had tremendous faith in Jesus because there's no record that any of them were unwilling to rip through someone else's roof to get to Him. • Jesus knows every thought and intention of the heart, forgives sins, and heals the impossible because He's God. • The scribes don't care about evidence. They only want to oppose Jesus no matter what He says and does.	• Whose home was Jesus in? • Why wouldn't the people let the paralytic through to get to Jesus? • Why did Jesus call the paralytic "Son," and tell him his sins were forgiven rather than immediately heal him (v. 5)? • Why did Mark note the scribes were sitting? • Was the scribes' question in verse 7 sincere or accusatorial?

Whenever you read the Bible, are you more likely to make assumptions or to ask clarifying questions? Are you a good question asker? I'm still training myself to ask clarifying questions and to watch for assumptions.

- Note in the following T-chart any assumptions the scribes might have had about Jesus.
- Note any assumptions Levi might have had about Jesus.
- What assumptions did you have about any of the individuals in the passage?

DAY ONE | 49

ASSUMPTIONS	CLARIFYING QUESTIONS

TRANSFORMATION

When Jesus forgave the paralytic's sins, the Jewish leaders rightly assumed He claimed to be God and wrongly assumed He wasn't. Jesus proved the truth. At His command, the once-paralyzed man picked up his mat and walked home. Rather than consider the mounting evidence of Jesus's true identity, the religious leaders took offense at Him and began plotting His death.

The culture of the day has always battled God's Word. If the Bible never conflicts with our natural human tendencies or understanding, we're probably misinterpreting it. Let's not be like the Pharisees or the toddler on the playground. Let's not ram our heads against the metal bars of wrong assumptions about God and His Word. Wrong assumptions lead to doubts about God, which lead to egregious sins and perhaps even to the worst sin—rejecting Christ forever.

A correct understanding of God's Word leads to every spiritual blessing. Let's move past our assumptions and humbly seek to know and understand the truth. God's Word establishes us in the truth, guards our hearts and minds from wrong assumptions, and makes our joy complete.

TRANSFORMATIONAL TRUTH

The truth sets us free. Anything else destroys.

Add to or review your Attributes of God list at the back of the book.

If you truly believe Jesus is who He proved He is in today's passage, how will you respond? What will it look like in your life to truly believe your sins are forgiven? How will your walk in Christ be different if you live like you're forgiven? Journal your response.

TRANSFORMATIONAL BIBLE STUDY PRINCIPLES

- ✓ Assumptions are thoughts or ideas we believe to be true without putting much, if any, thought to them.
- ✓ When you study the Bible, lay down your assumptions and examine—not cross-examine—God's Word through prayer, clarifying questions, and observation. Never put God's Word on trial.

MEMORY VERSE

Write out this week's memory verse and read it aloud five times.

Do your best to present yourself to God as one approved, a worker who has no need to be ashamed, rightly handling the word of truth. (2 Timothy 2:15)

WEEK TWO — *day two*

Context

TODAY'S READING

Mark 3:7–35

"Guess what, Bobby," my husband said to our son. "You're going to attend the elementary school down the street. To celebrate, we bought you a watch."

Bobby sat in somber silence. His two young sisters erupted into tears.

Seven-year-old Brittany begged, "Please let Bobby be homeschooled!"

Larry hugged Brittany while I comforted little Carolyn. Touched by such sibling love from a four-year-old, I asked her, "Why are you crying?"

"Bobby got a watch, and I didn't!"

To properly interpret what we see, we need the context—the full setting. As a homeschooled four-year-old, Carolyn didn't understand what "go to elementary school" meant, but she understood gifts. We'd just celebrated Christmas where everyone—including her—got presents. But not today.

Context matters.

CONTEXT MATTERS

The context of anything is its setting. Whether we realize it or not, we draw our understanding based on whatever context we know. If we want to understand Scripture's true sense (and avoid nonsense) we need to keep the text in its full context—its ancient context. We never want to "modernize" Scripture. Instead, let's step into the world of the Bible and think like the ancient Hebrews.

1. **Christ-centered context.** The Bible's overarching context is Christ. It's all about Him.
2. **Biblical context.** The Bible explains itself from its immediate context (the verse we're reading) to its broadest context (the whole Bible).
3. **Grammatical context.** Understanding the Bible requires us to consider what the author said and how he said it:
   - Writing styles (genre)
   - Writing techniques (literary devices)
   - Basic grammar
4. **Historical context.** The Bible happened in real time to real people throughout history.
5. **Cultural context.** The culture of biblical times and lands influenced how and why its people lived and acted as they did.

It takes time to learn the context of the whole Bible, but simply remembering that context matters reaps immediate rewards. We're less likely to rush to an interpretation—less likely to assume tears are about sibling love, not a watch.

Today, we'll look at the first two contexts: the Christ-centered context and the biblical context.

CHRIST-CENTERED CONTEXT

The Bible's overarching context is Christ. He's the context of everything, both in life and in Scripture. Jesus isn't the meaning of every verse, but the proclamation of His glory and salvation is the main point of the Bible.

In the Old Testament, we see Jesus through prophecies and through preincarnate appearances (aka *theophanies* or *Christophanies*). He's addressed by titles such as "the angel of the LORD" (Genesis 16:7) and "commander of the army of the LORD" (Joshua 5:14). With Moses before the burning bush, the preincarnate Jesus is identified as both the angel of the Lord and God (Exodus 3:1–6). The name by which God revealed Himself to Moses was "I AM" (Exodus 3:13–14). And in the New Testament, Jesus, with His seven "I Am" statements, identifies Himself as the I AM portrayed in the Old Testament (John 6:35–51; 8:12; 9:5; 10:7–9, 11–14; 11:25; 14:6; 15:1–5). As God, He received or commanded worship. God's angels always refuse worship (Revelation 19:10).

From Genesis to Revelation, the Bible speaks of Christ.

BIBLICAL CONTEXT

The Bible explains the Bible. Scholars call this the *synthesis principle*—Scripture interprets Scripture. Genesis helps explain Revelation. Zechariah, Daniel, and a few others help as well.

We can divide the biblical context into five levels, from its smallest (a single verse) to its broadest (the whole Bible):

1. The verse
2. Verses immediately before and after the verse
3. The entire chapter and book
4. Other books written by the same author
5. The whole Bible

Today we'll examine the text in its Christ-centered context and see how the biblical context helps us better understand a somewhat confusing verse in Mark.

PRACTICE SESSION: MARK 3:7–35

1. The verse

Write out Mark 3:12.

_____

_____

The question this verse raises is: Why does Jesus not want the demons to make Him known? When we consider only this one verse, we don't have enough context to answer this question. We need to widen the context.

2. Verses immediately before and after the verse

Read Mark 3:7–11 and 3:13–20.

What additional information do these passages provide that helps explain why Jesus silenced the demons?

_____

_____

_____

Let's widen the context further.

3. The entire chapter and book

Read Mark 3:20–35.

> Chapter: How does the context of chapter 3 help explain verse 12? (Consider vv. 23–30 and 35.)

_____

_____

_____

> Book: From when you read Mark last week, does any helpful context stand out in your memory?

_____

_____

4. Other books written by the same author

Mark didn't write any other books so we can skip this step.

5. The whole Bible

Draw from anything you already know from the whole Bible. How does this context help us understand why Jesus silenced the demons? Consider Genesis 3:1–5 and John 8:44.

_____

_____

TRANSFORMATION

In chapter 3, Jesus revealed He wasn't in league with Satan (Beelzebub) or Satan's dominion of demons. Instead, Jesus came to bind the "strong man" (Satan) (v. 27) and rob him of his possessions (his demon-possessed victims).

Throughout Mark, we see that Jesus came to defeat Satan's dominion, and He continually removes Himself from those who want to kill Him before the appointed time.

Scripture further reveals that Satan is the father of lies and the original twister of truth (Genesis 3:1–5; John 8:44). The demons imitate their leader, Satan. They submit to Jesus only because they have no choice. He's the king. They were trying to hurt Jesus, not glorify Him.

When we read through the Bible, we see it reveal that, from eternity to eternity, God controls every aspect of His plan and purposes. Jesus's and the Father's words and works testify to who Jesus is. Jesus doesn't need—or want—the lying mouths of demons to testify about Him.

Ignoring context can lead us to misunderstand what we read—or see, like I did with my four-year-old's tears over her brother's watch. Christ is the fullest context for everything, and His Word is the context for all truth. The Bible explains the motivations and desires of every heart—and it explains itself. Context matters.

TRANSFORMATIONAL TRUTH

Christ is the overarching context of everything in life and Scripture.

Add to or review your Attributes of God list at the back of the book.

If you truly believe every aspect of Jesus's earthly life was purposeful and aligned with God's eternal purposes, what will this look like in your life? How will recognizing the truths revealed in today's passage move you to trust Him with the challenges and uncertainties of your own life—particularly those that make no sense today or are especially agonizing? Journal your response.

_____
_____
_____
_____
_____
_____
_____
_____
_____
_____
_____
_____

TRANSFORMATIONAL BIBLE STUDY PRINCIPLES

- ✓ The Bible explains the motivations and desires of every heart—and it explains itself.
- ✓ The context of anything is its full setting.
- ✓ To understand Scripture's true sense (and avoid nonsense) keep the text in its full context:
    1. Christ-centered context
    2. Biblical context
    3. Grammatical context
    4. Historical context
    5. Cultural context

MEMORY VERSE: 2 TIMOTHY 2:15

Write out this week's memory verse.

WEEK TWO — day three

Genres

TODAY'S READING

Mark 4:1–34

"It's like putting lipstick on a pig." Whenever my architect husband says this, I know the pig. Someone somewhere wants him to renovate a hopeless, irredeemable fixer-upper. Larry is an outstanding architect but not a miracle worker. Christ is both. He turned this hopeless, irredeemable fixer-upper I call "me" into a temple of God.

"He who has ears to hear, let him hear" (Mark 4:9).

GRAMMATICAL CONTEXT

The Bible is rich with vivid phrases (although not phrases about pigs wearing lipstick). The writing styles (genres), techniques (literary devices), and grammar make the Bible a memorable masterpiece. When we understand its full grammatical context, the Bible's meaning opens up for us.

Genres are categories of writing styles such as *narrative*, *parables*, and *prophecy*. Each genre follows rules that guide how we read and interpret the text's meaning. Each book of the Bible typically contains a variety of genres.

Literary devices are creative writing techniques such as *idioms* and *parallelism* that are designed to enhance our understanding and memory of the text and its meaning.

Grammar is basic high school English—unless it's basic Hebrew or Greek. Grammar organizes words into meaningful sentences or phrases through word choices, verb tenses, punctuation, and all the other rules we learned in school and promptly forgot. Fortunately, scholars have created resources to tell us what we need to know.

In today's lesson, we'll examine one of Jesus's favorite communication styles: the genre *parables*, recorded in writing in the Gospels.

PARABLES

A parable lays a simple and relatable illustration from everyday life beside a spiritual truth to clarify its meaning. The spiritual truth's meaning reflects principles of the kingdom of God and leads the hearer to respond and reveal the true condition of his or her heart, whether it's full of faith or unbelief.

Jesus didn't tell parables to make truths easier to understand but rather, as He explains in today's passage, so insiders would understand and outsiders would not. Jesus designed His parables to reveal truth to those who have "ears to hear"—to listeners who respond in faith and obedience—and conceal truth from those who act like they don't have ears, who hear like people in the kingdom of darkness: deaf to truth and unwilling to listen.

The template for understanding all of Jesus's parables is the first parable in Mark—the parable of the soils. "He who has ears to hear, let him hear."

PRACTICE SESSION: MARK 4:1–34

The Parable of the Soils: Mark 4:1–9

INTENT

- Farmers in those days sowed the seeds before they plowed the fields.

TRUTH

Pray for ears to hear. Read Mark 4:1–9. Imagine you're sitting by the Sea of Galilee as Jesus shares this groundbreaking parable.

- For each soil in Mark 4:1–9, note the type of soil the seed falls onto and what happens to the seed. I'll start.

TRIUNE GOD	OTHERS
SEED	**SOIL**
The seed is the message of the kingdom of God: the gospel of Christ.	1. (v. 4) Hard path 2. (vv. 5–6) Rocky ground 3. (v. 7) 4. (v. 8)
	RESULTS
	1. Birds eat the seed. 2. 3. 4.

Jesus Explains the Parable of the Soils: Mark 4:10–20

Read Mark 4:10–20. Note the cause and result when God's Word is sown into human hearts. I'll start.

TRIUNE GOD	OTHERS
KINGDOM OF GOD	**SOIL/HEART**
The seed is the message of the kingdom of God: the gospel of Christ.	1. (v. 15) Hard path 2. (vv. 16–17) 3. (vv. 18–19) 4. (v. 20)
	RESULTS OF SOWING
	1. Satan immediately takes seed away. They hear the message but have no interest in the truth. 2. 3. 4.

DAY THREE | 63

- What spiritual truth does the parable of the soils emphasize?

_____

_____

- How does this spiritual truth reflect the kingdom of God?

_____

_____

- How does God call us to respond?

_____

_____

Christ illustrated how we enter the kingdom of God through the gospel in the parable of the soils. We see that each soil receives the seed (the gospel) by the farmer sowing the seed onto the soil (the gospel preached to the hearer's heart). The true nature of the soil (the heart) is revealed by whether the hearer truly accepts or ultimately rejects the gospel. True and lasting spiritual fruit is the evidence that their heart was tilled (made ready) by God's Spirit to hear and believe the gospel.

More Parables: Mark 4:21–34

Want to dig deeper? Use the parable of the soils and Jesus's explanation as your guide to study the other parables in today's passage.

TRANSFORMATION

Do you have ears to hear? Has the gospel of Jesus Christ taken root in the soil of your heart? If so, prepare to bear fruit—the fruit of righteousness and good works—through the Word of God implanted in your heart and through the power of God, who causes the growth.

When Christ transforms us, it's never like putting lipstick on a pig. Christ doesn't renovate us. He doesn't make us a better version of ourselves. He makes us a brand-new creation and a radiant reflection of Himself (Romans 8:29; 2 Corinthians 5:17). Who Christ redeems, He transforms (Philippians 1:6; 2:13). If you don't see a personal change, consider whether you've truly believed. If you have trusted in Christ, consider if you've been neglecting God's Word or resisting obeying it. Pray and ask God to reveal the truth of your heart.

TRANSFORMATIONAL TRUTH

When Christ redeems, fruitfulness follows.

Add to or review your Attributes of God list at the back of the book.

If you truly believe what today's passage reveals about Jesus and God's kingdom, how will you respond? What will it look like in your life to respond with ears that hear and to be fruitful? Journal your response.

_____

_____

_____

_____

_____

_____

_____

_____

_____

_____

_____

_____

_____

TRANSFORMATIONAL BIBLE STUDY PRINCIPLES

- ✓ When we understand the writing styles (genres), techniques (literary devices), and grammar, the Bible's meaning opens up for us.
- ✓ Parables lay a simple and relatable illustration from everyday life beside a spiritual truth to clarify its meaning. That truth reflects principles of the kingdom of God, leads the hearer to respond, and reveals the true condition of his or her heart.

MEMORY VERSE: 2 TIMOTHY 2:15

Write out this week's memory verse.

WEEK TWO — day four

Grammar

TODAY'S READING

Mark 4:35–5:20

"Bobby, apologize to your sister for pushing her."
  Tears in the corners of my five-year-old's eyes threatened to spill over, but he stood stone still.
  Was my normally compliant son truly refusing to apologize?
  Lord, what's going on in Bobby's heart? Why won't he apologize? Wait. Could it be?
  "Bobby, do you know what the word *apologize* means?"
  Nearly wailing, he cried, "No!"
  I laughed and reworded my instructions, which he quickly obeyed. Words have meaning. We need to know their intended meaning.

WORDS HAVE MEANING

The power of each author's word choices is not just in *what* they say but also in *how* they say it. By the Holy Spirit's direction, each biblical author selected his words carefully to convey the exact meaning he intended his readers to understand. Let's not modernize the original intended meaning.
  The diligent work of translators allows us to read those authors' messages in our language, but remember, we're not reading their original words. Our translation can miss some of the power and nuances of the original ancient Hebrew, Greek, and Aramaic—especially if we read too fast.
  My seventh-grade teacher taught me to focus on the whole sentence as I read rather than Reading. One. Word. At. A. Time. Her advice made me a more fluid reader. Now I'm telling you to do the opposite

because studying is different from reading. When we study the Bible, we want to Notice. Each. Word.

FIVE TIPS FOR NOTICING. EACH. WORD.

1. Notice verbs and nouns—especially repeated ones.
   - What do the repeated words highlight?
   - Who's doing the action? Who's receiving it?
   - Is the verb past, present, or future tense?
   - Are the nouns singular or plural?
2. Don't miss the seemingly insignificant words like *on, when, to, in, as, into, because,* and *and.* Teachers call them conjunctions and prepositions. You can call them thingamabobs as long as you notice them and why they're there. Thingamabobs are like lights on a staircase. They keep us from missing steps in the story's forward progression.
3. Pay attention to sentence types.
   - Is the sentence *declarative* (also called *indicative*)—a statement of truth, teaching, or information?
   - Is the sentence an *imperative*—a command to obey?
   - Is the sentence a *direct* question (which expects an answer) or a *rhetorical* question (which expects a response)?
4. Consider nuances of meaning.
   - Many words have multiple meanings. Some authors chose words for their double meaning or as a play on words in the original language. The translations don't always catch these nuances.
   - Be careful not to force an unintended meaning into the text. We want to interpret the original meaning, not invent new ones. (Consult a free online *1828 Webster Dictionary* or a Bible dictionary for more faithful word interpretations.)
5. Read the passages in different Bible translations.
   - Some good options are English Standard Version (ESV), New American Standard Bible (NASB), Legacy Standard Bible (LSB) Christian Standard Bible (CSB), Berean Study Bible (BSB), New King James Version (NKJV), New International Version (NIV), or New Living Translation (NLT).

- Biblehub.com offers multiple translations you can read side-by-side.

PRACTICE SESSION: MARK 4:35–41

INTENT

- To find the original Greek or Hebrew words, you can use a free online Strong's concordance. (Visit the *Discovering God's Word* tab at JeanWilund.com for links to free online concordances.)

TRUTH

Pray and read Mark 4:35–41. White-knuckle your boat oars as the storm winds slap your face and the waves flood over the gunwales and soak your feet. Pause at Mark's repeated words and ideas. Notice the seemingly insignificant words—the thingamabobs—and the nuances of meaning. Use all five tips as you study Mark's word choices in today's passage.

TRIUNE GOD	OTHERS

- Mark used the word "great" (*megas*) three times.

    Megas means "large, great, in the widest sense."[4]
    – a great windstorm (v. 37)
    – a great calm (v. 39)
    – great fear (v. 41)

    Compare and contrast these three phrases in their context. What does Mark spotlight about Jesus and His disciples?

    _____
    _____
    _____
    _____
    _____

- Mark used two words in today's passage to indicate fear.

    Deilos means "afraid, timid, fearful."[5] (v. 40)

    Phobeó means "fear, to put to flight, to terrify, frighten" and also "to reverence, venerate, to treat with deference or reverential obedience."[6] (v. 41)

- Compare and contrast how Mark uses *deilos* fear (v. 40) and *phobeó* fear (v. 41) to reveal truths about Jesus and the disciples' faith. If they believe in who Christ is, why should they be afraid when Christ is with them?

    _____
    _____
    _____
    _____

- Jesus speaks, and the truth of who He is strikes the disciples' hearts as they watch creation obey Him. Quaking in their wet sandals, the disciples are filled with "great fear." Write out Mark 4:41.

___

- When was the last time Jesus could have asked you why you're so *deilos*—so afraid? Do you still lack confidence in Him and His power? Do your circumstances still feel greater than Jesus? Did Jesus seem as if He didn't care or was asleep while life threatened to drag you under? Journal your thoughts.

___

Want to dig deeper? Pray and read Mark 4:42–5:20. Jesus has rescued you from the deadly storm, but now He's brought you to a violent crazy man. Study this passage using the five tips above. (Hint: Notice any form of the word *beg*. Who's begging? What is it they're begging for, and why? What does their begging reveal about their understanding of Jesus?)

TRIUNE GOD	OTHERS

TRANSFORMATION

The moment my son learned the meaning of the word *apologize*, he responded quickly and hugged his sister so tightly she almost fell over. Every word of Scripture is designed to lead us to respond quickly to the truth of who Christ is.

Jesus speaks, and the winds and waves obey. He commands, and a legion of cowering demons unwillingly submits. When we truly understand who Christ is, great fear—reverent fear—will consume us. We'll throw ourselves before His throne of grace and beg forgiveness for the great windstorm of our sins and doubts. In Him, we'll find mercy and a great calm of abiding peace and joy.

TRANSFORMATIONAL TRUTH

Reverent fear of Christ calms all other fears.

Add to or review your Attributes of God list at the back of the book.

What will it look like if you truly fear Christ with reverential fear? What storm will be stilled in your heart or home? What *deilos* fear will be cast out? Journal your response.

TRANSFORMATIONAL BIBLE STUDY PRINCIPLES

- ✓ Notice *what* the authors say and *how* they say it.
- ✓ When you study the Bible, Notice. Each. Word.
- ✓ Notice verbs and nouns—especially repeated ones.
- ✓ Don't miss the thingamabob words.
- ✓ Pay attention to sentence types.
- ✓ Consider nuances of meaning.
- ✓ Read the passages in different Bible translations.

MEMORY VERSE: 2 TIMOTHY 2:15

Write out this week's memory verse.

WEEK TWO — day five

Writing Styles

TODAY'S READING

Mark 5:21–43

It wasn't one of my brighter moments.

A friend and I were chatting about our favorite Bible authors whom we'd come to know and love like old friends. I extoled Paul's wisdom in the book of James. She agreed.

Swept away in the excitement of our conversation, it took us a moment to realize we gave Paul credit for James's writing. In our defense, Paul wrote most of the New Testament. But he didn't write James. James wrote James.

UNIQUE WRITING STYLES

The Bible authors' writing reflected their personalities, but they chose the styles and techniques that best proclaimed the message God directed them to write. Nothing is random.

Mark wrote a Roman-styled, fast-paced narrative. One of his favorite words was *immediately*. He also had a taste for chiasms and for one writing technique so distinctive it's named after him: the Markan Sandwich.

THE MARKAN SANDWICH AND ITS COUSIN CHIASM

A *Markan Sandwich* is a story sandwiched between two interrupted halves of another story. The second half of the story picks up where the first half left off after the middle event spotlights the message, spiritual truth, or common theme of the sandwich. The two events relate to each other and help interpret each other.

A *chiasm* is a writing technique that presents events, ideas, or truths and then repeats them in reverse order (ABBA). For example, Matthew 20:16 (BSB):

A^1—So the last
    B^1—will be first,
    B^2—and the first
A^2—will be last

Chiasms can be one-liners or may span entire chapters. The center of a chiasm spotlights the message.

Mark is full of chiasms and at least six Markan Sandwiches (Mark 3:20–35; 5:21–43; 6:7–30; 11:12–25; 14:1–11; and 14:53–72). We'll examine my favorite Sandwich today.

PRACTICE SESSION: MARK 5:21–43

INTENT

- Jairus was a respected Jewish ruler in the synagogue. He surely knew the religious leaders' hatred of Jesus. They didn't hide their contempt.
- A Jewish woman with a bleeding disorder would have been considered unclean and thus ostracized from contact with her religious community. Anyone who touched her or entered her home became unclean (Leviticus 15:19–31; Ezekiel 36:17).
- Many believed the clothing of healers held healing power.
- Touching a dead body made a person ceremonially unclean.
- The Jews hired professional mourners to wail. The rules that regulated their funerals stated: "Even the poorest man of the Jewish people may not provide fewer than two flutes and a lamenting woman, which it was customary to hire for a funeral, as these too are included in the duties of burial" (Rabbi Yehuda in Mishna Ketubot 4:4).[7]

TRUTH

Pray and then read Mark 5:21–43. Feel the intensity of Jairus's urgency. His daughter is dying. Feel the desperation of the unclean woman. She's destitute of money, community, and hope. Examine Jesus as He reveals more about who He is. Consider the Truth questions as you make notes in the T-chart. I'll start.

TRIUNE GOD	OTHERS
JESUS	**JAIRUS**
• Jesus can heal with just a word . . . yet He goes with Jairus to his daughter. Why? • Jesus knows all things . . . but He asks who touched Him. Why? Why does it matter?	• Respected Jewish leader • Helpless
	DAUGHTER
	• Low in social status—a deceased female child • Helpless
	WOMAN
	• Low in social status: unclean, rejected, poor, a woman • Helpless

- What risk does Jairus take to come to Jesus?

_____

_____

- Consider the cultural context. Imagine how Jairus feels when Jesus stops to help an unclean woman while his daughter is dying.

_____

_____

DAY FIVE | 77

- What does the woman most likely believe causes her healing (v. 28)?

_____

_____

- What truth about her healing does she need to know (v. 34)?

_____

_____

- What name does Jesus call her? Why do you think He calls her by this name (v. 34)?

_____

_____

- Immediately after Jesus sends her off in peace, Jairus receives word that his daughter is dead. How does Jesus respond (v. 36)?

_____

_____

- How old is Jairus's daughter (v. 42)? _____

- How long has the woman been bleeding (v. 25)? _____

- What spiritual truths do these two events reveal? (Remember, they interpret each other.)

_____

_____

TRANFORMATION

Each of the Bible's authors—James, Paul, Mark, and the rest—used their writing styles to bring us to God, proclaim the excellencies of our Lord, and move us to greater faith.

Mark sandwiched the account of the woman who bled physically and financially for twelve agonizing years in the middle of the pleading of a prominent synagogue ruler whose twelve-year-old daughter was dying. No one but Jesus could save them. The law couldn't save them. It declared the woman unclean. The law was powerless to save Jairus's daughter from death.

Both Jairus and the woman came to Jesus with great faith. He called them to greater faith to show them more clearly who He is. He's not simply Jesus the Healer. He's their Creator and Savior—their Messiah.

Jesus counted their faith as righteousness, removed their sin and shame, and made them beloved sons and daughters (Romans 4:1–21; Ephesians 2:8–9; 1 John 3:1).

Do not fear, only believe.

TRANSFORMATIONAL TRUTH

Do not fear, only believe.

Add to or review your Attributes of God list at the back of the book.

If you truly believe Christ's supremacy, power, and compassion, as this Markan Sandwich reveals, what will it look like in your life? How is Jesus calling you to even greater faith today? Journal your response.

_____
_____
_____
_____
_____
_____
_____
_____
_____
_____

TRANSFORMATIONAL BIBLE STUDY PRINCIPLES

- ✓ The Bible authors' writing reflected their personalities, but they chose the styles and techniques that best proclaimed the message God directed them to write. Nothing is random.
- ✓ A *Markan Sandwich* is a story sandwiched between two interrupted halves of another story. The middle event spotlights the message, spiritual truth, or common theme of the sandwich. The two events relate to each other and help interpret each other.
- ✓ A *chiasm* is a writing technique that presents events, ideas, or truths and then repeats them in reverse order (ABBA).

MEMORY VERSE: 2 TIMOTHY 2:15

Write out this week's memory verse.

WEEK THREE

Eyes to See

MARK 6:1–8:38

Open my eyes, that I may behold wondrous things out of your law.
—Psalm 119:18

WEEK THREE — day one

Historical Context

TODAY'S READING

Mark 6:1–29

Have you thought about the fact that neither time nor history existed until God spoke the first word of creation?

Time is the progress of events in history. History is the record of events that happened in time. Without time, there's no history. There's only God the Father, Son, and Holy Spirit existing in perfect unity outside of time.

If this thought doesn't break your brain, it ought to at least wrench it a little.

HISTORICAL CONTEXT MATTERS

The events in the Bible happened in real time to real people. Their history impacted them just as our history impacts how we live, think, and understand God's Word. Questions like the following help us keep the historical context in mind.

- When did the author's audience live, and what was happening in his world when the events in the passage took place?
- Did the original audience live before, during, or after major life-changing events such as the exodus from Egypt, the Babylonian captivity, or the cross and resurrection of Christ?
- Who were the government and leaders of the original audience or surrounding nations, and what were they like?
- For additional historical context, consult Scripture, commentaries, study Bibles, Bible encyclopedias, and biblical resource websites.

We have the whole Bible for historical context, but most of the Bible's original audience didn't. To understand each author's message the way his original audience would have, consider only the Scriptures they had. When Mark wrote, the only other New Testament book available was most likely Galatians.[8]

Nothing in Scripture is random. Whenever an author provides historical context, he intends the context to help direct the Scripture's interpretation—including today's passage.

PRACTICE SESSION: MARK 6:1–29

Mark 6:1–13

INTENT

- Jesus was born in Bethlehem but raised in Nazareth—a city noted in the Bible with scorn. "Can anything good come out of Nazareth?" (Matthew 2:1, 23; John 1:45–46).
- Jesus visited Nazareth earlier in His ministry. The residents took offense at His message and tried to hurl Him off a cliff. He walked away instead (Luke 4:16–30).
- The Old Testament records Israel's long and violent history of not honoring God's prophets. They often mocked, ignored, persecuted, or killed the prophets God sent to warn them.

TRUTH

Pray and read Mark 6:1–13. Return with Jesus to His hometown, but don't expect a parade. Hear Jesus's wisdom. Feel Nazareth's scorn. Travel through the villages with the disciples as they follow Jesus's example and by His authority preach the gospel, heal the sick, and cast out demons. Make notes as you consider the Truth questions and the historical context. I'll start.

TRIUNE GOD	OTHERS
JESUS	**NAZARETH**
<ul><li>Hometown—Nazareth</li><li>Taught in synagogue</li><li>Isaiah 6:9—prophets not honored in hometown</li><li>Performed few miracles—Nazareth's unbelief</li><li>*Marveled* over their unbelief</li></ul>	<ul><li>*Astonished* at Jesus's ideas, wisdom, miracles</li><li>*Offended* by Jesus</li></ul>
	DISCIPLES
	<ul><li>Watching Jesus and learning</li></ul>

- What did Jesus accomplish by going to Nazareth? (Hint: Remember how Jesus has been preparing His disciples. He shows and tells continually.)

Mark 6:14–29

INTENT

- All six of the Herods in the Bible reflect the evil character of the first, Herod the Great, who tried to kill young Jesus by slaughtering the baby boys in Bethlehem.
- The Herod in today's passage, King Herod Antipas, stole his brother Herod Philip's wife, Herodias. She divorced Philip to marry Antipas, who divorced his wife to marry her. Herodias was also Antipas's niece. What a mess.

TRUTH

Pray and read Mark 6:14–29. Jesus's disciples tour the land performing miracles and casting out demons. Herod throws a feast. If you can stomach it, grab a seat and watch Herod's horror show. Keep the Truth questions in mind, look for evidence of any of the three persons of our triune God in the passage, and take notes in the chart.

TRIUNE GOD	OTHERS
	JOHN
	KING HEROD
	HERODIAS/DAUGHTER

- Mark 1:14 barely mentions John's arrest. How does Mark's detailed account in today's passage give us the historical context we need to understand his main point concerning John's arrest and execution? Consider that Herod didn't want John to die. He feared John as a holy and righteous man. He enjoyed listening to him.

_____
_____
_____
_____

TRANSFORMATION

Nazareth took offense at Jesus's message and authority.

Because John the Baptist declared Antipas's actions unlawful, Herodias took offense at John and jumped at the chance to declare, "Off with his head!"

The message of Christ has always offended those who don't have ears to hear because the gospel confronts us with our sin. Pride is the root—and fuel—of sin. Jesus is the cure.

The gospel of Jesus is the gospel of love, grace, and mercy. Even with the response Jesus knew He'd receive in Nazareth, He chose to return to offer the gospel. Jesus's family and many lost souls lived in Nazareth. He came to live and die and destroy the power of sin, Satan, and death for lost souls.

Jesus spent three years showing and telling His disciples to prepare them to experience the same kind of rejection He received in Nazareth—and worse, like John—for the gospel.

We'll all die someday. For those who believe in Christ, the best is ahead. The Lover of our soul waits for us. Until then, none of us are exempt from suffering for Christ. Do not fear or let pride tarnish your message by being offended when others hate you. Only believe. What our enemies and Satan intend for evil, God has always intended, and accomplishes, for good.

One day God will bring an end to all His children's suffering. He'll redeem our sorrows and wipe away every tear from our eyes. Death, mourning, crying, and pain will be no more (Revelation 21:4). God already wrote this glorious future—*your* glorious future—before time and history began.

TRANSFORMATIONAL TRUTH

Pride is the root—and fuel— of sin. Jesus is the cure.

Add to or review your Attributes of God list at the back of the book.

If you truly believe the truths God's Word reveals in today's passage, how will you respond? How will you face persecution when it comes? What will it look like for you to respond like Christ when those who should love you oppose you? Journal your response.

_____
_____
_____
_____
_____
_____
_____
_____
_____
_____
_____
_____
_____
_____

TRANSFORMATIONAL BIBLE STUDY PRINCIPLES
- ✓ The events in the Bible happened in real time to real people. Historical context matters.
- ✓ For additional historical context, consult Scripture, commentaries, study Bibles, Bible encyclopedias, and biblical resource websites.

MEMORY VERSE

Write out this week's memory verse and recite it five times.

Open my eyes, that I may behold
wondrous things out of your law.
(Psalm 119:18)

WEEK THREE — day two

Cultural Context

TODAY'S READING

Mark 6:30–56

Did you know that if sheep fall onto their back, they can't get up on their own? They'll die within hours. I know streetlights pop on automatically when the sun goes down, but the shepherding culture is utterly foreign to this city girl.

CULTURE INFLUENCES BEHAVIOR

Culture is the way a society lives. It includes the people's beliefs, customs, and lifestyle.

Every society has a distinct culture that explains their behavior and influences their choices. The people pick up their society's culture, often without even realizing it unless they determine not to conform.

When God created the nation of Israel, He set them apart from the rest of the world and gave them a unique culture to teach them—and through them, the rest of the world—about Himself and His salvation. He called them to abstain from absorbing the neighboring nations' cultures and remain true to His teachings and commands.

When we study the Bible, our job isn't to judge the culture we're reading about. Rather, we're to try to understand that culture so we can better understand the text. Asking questions like the following will help us.

- What cultural norms did God establish for His people?
- What cultural norms did the other nations embrace?
- How and what did the people in the passage worship?

- Did those in the passage live among their own people or in a foreign land and culture?

Sometimes the authors revealed the cultural context, but they often assumed the reader already knew it. Since Mark wrote to Roman Gentiles, he explained some of the Jewish culture. To learn more cultural context, we can turn to study Bibles, Bible encyclopedias, commentaries, and biblical resource websites.

Today, we'll see how knowing cultural context helps us better understand the passage's meaning. I gathered much of the cultural context about today's passage from biblical resources.

PRACTICE SESSION: MARK 6:30–56

Mark 6:30–44

INTENT

- Shepherding had long been a common profession among God's people.
- God wove the theme of the Lord as our Good Shepherd throughout the Bible, notably in Psalm 23, which echoes in parts of today's passage.
- Bread and smoked or dried fish were common in Jesus's day, especially along the sea.
- Since food wasn't abundant, only the wealthy ate until they were "satisfied"—in other words, stuffed.

Pray and read Mark 6:30–44. Imagine you're one of the disciples. Jesus takes you by boat to a quiet place to rest, but when you approach the shore, a crowd rushes from the wide, green pastures to Jesus like sheep to their shepherd.

Remember the Truth questions and make notes in the T-chart as you study.

TRIUNE GOD	OTHERS
	CROWDS
	DISCIPLES

- How familiar are you with the shepherding culture? Did you instinctively recognize the comparison between today's passage and Psalm 23, or did you need the comparison pointed out?

_____
_____

- Jesus immediately fed His "sheep" what they needed most. What did He feed them? (See v. 34.)

_____
_____

- Mark records that the people "ate and were satisfied" (Mark 6:42). The original Greek word for "satisfied" (*chortazō*) means "to gorge or supply food in abundance."[9] What does this teach us about Jesus and His care for His sheep—including us?

_____

_____

_____

Mark 6:45–56

INTENT

- The Jewish day was divided into two twelve-hour shifts and counted from sunset to sunset.
- The Roman day was divided into two twelve-hour shifts but started at midnight. The Romans also kept time using four "watches": first (6:00 p.m.–9:00 p.m.); second (9:00 p.m.–12:00 a.m.); third (12:00 a.m.–3:00 a.m.); fourth (3:00 a.m.–6:00 a.m.).
- A belief in ghosts was prevalent in the first century.
- The people believed healing powers flowed from a healer's clothing.

TRUTH

Pray and read Mark 6:45–56. Climb into the boat with the other disciples as Jesus sends you off without Him. In the middle of the night, squint at what appears to be a man—or a ghost!—walking on the water. Feel terror consume you. Notice everything Jesus says and does.

Remember the Truth questions and make notes in the T-chart as you study.

TRIUNE GOD	OTHERS
	CROWDS
	DISCIPLES

The disciples saw Jesus, the Good Shepherd, do the impossible. He fed five thousand–plus "sheep." But when the storm hit, His disciples defaulted to their cultural beliefs, which inclined them to believe the man walking on the water must be a ghost, not their miracle-working Lord.

We're always being trained what to think and believe through our culture, environment, what we read and listen to, as well as the people we spend time with. We must train ourselves to know and believe the truth—God's Word; otherwise we'll believe the subliminal training that comes with living on earth.

- When trouble arises, how quickly does doubt haunt you despite what you know about God?

- As your knowledge of Christ grows, in what ways is your faith deepening? What is some of the evidence?

TRANSFORMATION

Jesus is the Good Shepherd (John 10:11). He makes us lie down in green pastures and leads us beside quiet waters. But in the presence of our enemies, we often forget everything we've learned about Christ. We know who He is and what He's done, but in the storm, we don't recognize Jesus or His power. We tremble despite the loaves. We don't truly understand. Jesus's power is endless. His love is matchless. He sees us in every watch of the day and has promised to never leave us.

Will we trust Him?

TRANSFORMATIONAL TRUTH

No matter how much culture or history changes, Christ remains the same.

Add to or review your Attributes of God list at the back of the book.

If you truly believe what today's passage reveals about Jesus, what will this look like in your life? When a storm rises, how will you respond? What will it look like for you to jump out of the boat and run to Christ on the water of great faith, like Peter did (Matthew 14:28–29), rather than forget what you know about Him and tremble in the storm? Journal your response.

_____
_____
_____
_____
_____
_____
_____
_____
_____
_____
_____
_____

_____

_____

_____

_____

TRANSFORMATIONAL BIBLE STUDY PRINCIPLES

- ✓ Culture explains societies' behaviors and influences their choices. Seek to understand the cultures to better understand the text.
- ✓ The Bible often reveals the cultural context. Study Bibles, Bible encyclopedias, commentaries, and biblical resource websites can provide more information.

MEMORY VERSE: PSALM 119:18

Write out this week's memory verse.

WEEK THREE — *day three*

Doctrine

TODAY'S READING

Mark 7:1–37

"Let's just turn around and go back the way we came."

We'd been hiking almost three hours with our three young children. Our path now ran through the top of a rushing waterfall with no guardrails to keep us from being swept over the edge.

My husband's solution was for him to carry each child, one by one, through the water to the other side.

My solution would have been to build a steel bridge over the waterfall, add two levels of guardrails, then tie a rope around each kid and anchor them all to a giant oak tree just in case.

I wonder if this is how the Jewish leaders felt when they added layers upon layers of rules to the doctrines of God so His people couldn't possibly get washed over the waterfall of disobedience.

THE BIBLE DETERMINES DOCTRINE

Doctrine is the Bible's teachings that direct how we're to think and live like Christ. For example, the doctrine of God explains what the Bible teaches about His character, nature, and ways. The doctrine of sanctification explains what the Bible teaches about the purpose, means, and methods God uses to make us like Christ.

We step onto dangerous ground whenever we let the culture or our personal preferences determine our doctrine, or when we take one or a few verses of Scripture and shape an entire doctrine around them. No matter how well-intentioned we may be, the whole Bible, and the Bible alone, must shape our doctrine.

When the whole Bible shapes our doctrine, the Bible's doctrines shape us into the image of Christ. We guard ourselves against being "tossed to and fro by the waves and carried about by every wind of doctrine" (Ephesians 4:14). As Paul warns, "The time is coming when people will not endure sound teaching, but having itching ears they will accumulate for themselves teachers to suit their own passions, and will turn away from listening to the truth and wander off into myths" (2 Timothy 4:3–4).

God's Word is our perfect guardrail to keep us safe from every false teaching. Know the Word. Know the Word. Know the Word.

The scribes and Pharisees added to God's Word to protect the people from disobedience. The guardrails they added around Scripture displayed their unbelief in the sufficiency of God's Word to do its perfect work in the people's hearts. Jesus confronts the Pharisees' sin of unbelief and Scripture tampering in today's passage.

PRACTICE SESSION: MARK 7:1–37

Mark 7:1–23

INTENT

- The scribes and Pharisees were the interpreters and teachers of God's law. They added hundreds of man-made rules, the "tradition of the elders," to God's perfect law to protect Israel from even the idea of breaking one of God's laws—except when it came to plotting Jesus's murder, of course. They elevated their traditions to equal status with God's law. (See Matthew 23.)
- *Corban* is the tradition of dedicating—not necessarily giving—something to God by a vow.
- The people in the first century didn't have copies of Scripture. They had to trust their religious leaders.

TRUTH

Pray and read Mark 7:1–23. Stand with Jesus as the Pharisees and scribes rebuke Him for letting His disciples ignore their elders' traditions. Listen to Jesus's strong response and learn. Remember the Truth questions as you make notes in the T-chart.

TRIUNE GOD	OTHERS
	PHARISEES/CROWDS
	DISCIPLES

- What does Jesus call the religious leaders in verse 6? _____

- Isaiah spoke of the leaders in Jesus's day and also of false teachers today. What is your confidence level in being able to spot whether a teaching you hear is true biblical doctrine or the opinion of the speaker?

_____
_____
_____

- If Christ were to reveal your true heart, what might He say? In what way(s) might you honor God with your lips more than your heart? (Pray for forgiveness, rest in His love, and seek to know and love Him with your whole heart.)

_____
_____
_____
_____
_____

Mark 7:24–37

INTENT

- A Gentile is anyone who's not Jewish.
- Jewish traditions didn't allow Jews to enter Gentile homes.
- Jews called Gentiles "dogs" because they weren't God's children. When Jesus used the term, He wasn't being derogatory. He was using it as a metaphor, which the Syrophoenician woman understood. She responded by calling Him "Lord," or master. She recognized His spiritual authority.
- Both God and His Word place great value on women. The first-century culture devalued women.
- Communication with someone who has both a hearing and speech impairment requires visual methods.
- The region of Decapolis is a gentile region.
- Sickness was seen by the Jews as a sign of God's displeasure.

TRUTH

Pray and read Mark 7:24–37. Follow Jesus as He displays what He taught through two powerful visuals. Remember the Truth questions and Jesus's humble and compassionate nature as you study and make notes in the T-chart. Compare this passage to Jesus's earlier message in Mark 7:1–23.

TRIUNE GOD	OTHERS

TRANSFORMATION

When we remain faithful to Christ and His doctrines rather than add to or take away from His Word and teachings, we'll walk through even the most raging trials in safety. Like my husband, who carried each of our children through the waterfall with ease, we can trust God's Word to carry us safely to the truth rather than over the waterfall of every wrong belief and doctrine.

Ignorance of the Bible's doctrines is cured by studying the Bible—the whole Bible. Unbelief in the Bible's doctrines is cured by dying to our pride, to thinking we know better than God what biblical doctrine should or should not be.

TRANSFORMATIONAL TRUTH

When the whole Bible shapes our doctrine, the Bible's doctrines shape us into the image of Christ. Know the Word. Know the Word. Know the Word.

Add to or review your Attributes of God list at the back of the book.

What will it look like if you truly believe the truths Jesus taught in today's passage? How will you study biblical doctrine and evaluate the beliefs you already hold and those taught by others? What will it look like to truly trust in Scripture's sufficiency? Journal your response.

_____

_____

_____

_____

_____

_____

_____

_____

TRANSFORMATIONAL BIBLE STUDY PRINCIPLES

- ✓ Doctrine is the teachings of the Bible that explain how we're to think and live like Christ (Ephesians 4:11–16).
- ✓ The whole Bible alone, not our culture and personal preferences, determines doctrine.
- ✓ God's Word is our perfect guardrail to keep us safe from false teachings.

MEMORY VERSE: PSALM 119:18

Write out this week's memory verse.

WEEK THREE — day four

Structure

TODAY'S READING
Mark 8:1–30

I'd misplaced my husband again. "Where's Dad?" I asked my son.

Bobby pointed across the Florida hotel lobby. "He's in the corner staring at the ceiling."

Such is life with an architect.

Larry is obsessed with every aspect of a building's structure. Perhaps that's because without proper structure, buildings fall down. Or less extreme, people get lost—like when I traveled to Ruthin, Wales, a year later with my dad.

Dad and I stayed in a renovated castle. Part of this hotel's charm was its incomprehensible web of hallways. We had to drop breadcrumbs whenever we left our room to find our way back.

BIBLICAL STRUCTURE

Writing, like buildings, has structure—even if its structure is incomprehensible. Since God is a God of order (1 Corinthians 14:33), we can be certain He gave the Bible a well-ordered structure to lead us to the truths He wants us to know. This fact doesn't mean we'll always recognize or understand the structure at first.

The Bible's authors filled its pages with various structure types such as parables and parallelism. Whenever a book or passage seems unstructured or random, it's a clue that either the author is using the seeming randomness to grab our attention, or we're so off the intended path that we need to follow breadcrumbs back and find the intended structure.

HOW TO FIND THE STRUCTURE

The following questions can help us find the author's structure.

What genres did the author use? The authors chose genres whose structures best helped lead the reader to his intended message.

What kinds of questions did the author ask? Rhetorical, imperative, and direct questions may simply be part of a normal dialogue, or they may be the structure the author or speaker chose to lead to an intended conclusion.

Did the author present lists? If so, is the list's order random, or is it organized from lesser to greater or vice versa? Is the list a genealogy? If so, God is about to do something new and big (Genesis 5; Exodus 6:14–27; Luke 3:23–38). Most lists are representative, not exhaustive, such as Paul's list of the fruit of the Spirit (Galatians 5:22–23).

Where are the turning points and hinges in his book? Turning points dramatically shift the action or attitudes into a new direction. Hinges flip the script into a no-turning-back direction. We'll learn more about these in our next lesson.

Did the author use repetition? Parallelism and chiasms are two popular forms of repetition—the repeating of similar or contrasting words, ideas, or events. Repetition was one of Mark's favorite structures, as we'll see in today's passage.

PRACTICE SESSION: MARK 8:1–30

Mark used two parallel series of intentional events to spotlight spiritual truths from and about Christ.
- Rather than a Truth chart, today's chart displays the parallel events. Our goal is to discern how these two series highlight the same overarching spiritual truths.
- Keep the Intent and Truth questions in mind as you **pray and read Mark 8:1–30.**

PASSAGE IN MARK	SERIES OF EVENTS	PASSAGE IN MARK
6:31–44	← (Fed 5,000+ Jews) **Feeding multitudes—Jesus cares for His sheep** (Fed 4,000+ Gentiles) →	8:1–9
6:45–56	← (Jesus walked on water; sailed from Jewish to gentile region) **Crossing the sea—Jesus is in control** (Sailed from gentile region to Jewish region) →	8:10
7:1–23	← (The elders exalt their traditions over God's law) **Jesus conflicts with Pharisees** (The Pharisees demand a sign) →	8:11–13
7:24–30	← (Conversation reveals Gentiles' humble faith) **Conversation about bread** (Conversation reveals Pharisees' pride) →	8:14–21
7:31–36	← (Gentile: Jesus heals deaf and mute man) **Jesus gives physical and spiritual healing** (Jewish: Jesus heals blind man in stages) →	8:22–26
7:37	← (Gentile crowd confesses Jesus "has done all things well") **Confession about Jesus** (Peter confesses Jesus is the Messiah) →	8:27–30

- Mark compares and contrasts interactions between Jesus and the Jewish leaders (God's own leaders) with interactions with Gentiles. What are the results and overarching spiritual truths Mark reveals through these two series?

_____
_____
_____
_____

- How do humility and pride influence how these people see Jesus? And themselves?

- The humble will see Jesus revealed; the proud will see their own shame exposed. How might pride be causing spiritual blindness in your own life? Pray for more humility.

TRANSFORMATION

Apart from Jesus, we cannot find the path to salvation or to sanctification—to becoming like Christ. We'd be as lost as my dad and I were in the incomprehensible hallways of our Welsh castle-hotel. Through two series of similar events, Jesus mercifully and repeatedly showed His disciples the way they must walk if they were to one day shepherd His flock (the church) with humble compassion rather than Pharisaical pride. If we don't learn to follow Christ in faith and humility like His faithful disciples, we'll follow the path that leads to destruction and shame.

The disciples had Jesus to lead them. We have His well-structured Word and the Holy Spirit as our wise and merciful guide. Step by step, He will lead us to find and follow Scripture's structure into all truth.

TRANSFORMATIONAL TRUTH

If we don't learn to follow Christ in faith and humility, we'll follow the path to destruction and shame.

Add to or review your Attributes of God list at the back of the book.

If you truly believe the truths revealed in today's passage, what will it look like in your life? In what areas and ways do you need to die to your pride? How will you show humility in dealing with others and in your worship of Christ? What will you confess about Jesus? Journal your response.

TRANSFORMATIONAL BIBLE STUDY PRINCIPLES

- ✓ The biblical authors chose the structure for their writings that best leads us to the truth God wants to know. Find and follow the structure.
- ✓ Each event in a repeated series works together to highlight overarching spiritual truths.

MEMORY VERSE: PSALM 119:18

Write out this week's memory verse.

WEEK THREE — *day five*

Turning Points

TODAY'S READING

Mark 8:22–38

How many turning points have you had in your life? I've had so many, it's a wonder I haven't wound up back where I started. For every true believer, the moment of our salvation is the hinge in our life—the moment when everything changed. We were dead, and now we live.

The hinge of history is the death and resurrection of Jesus Christ. He died and rose again so we may live forever.

THE PURPOSE OF TURNING POINTS IN SCRIPTURE

Turning points or hinges are a type of structure the biblical authors use to emphasize spiritual truth and move the reader to a specific response.

Each book tends to have one or more major turning points—hinges that change everything.

HOW TO FIND TURNING POINTS

The following questions help us recognize turning points.

- What moment or truth has this book been building up to?
- At what point in this book did God change in how He dealt with His people?
- When did the people change in how they responded to God?
- At what point does the author's writing move us in a decidedly different direction?
- How does this change point us to Jesus, the overarching theme of the Bible?

In books with lots of narrative (such as the history books or Gospels), it can be easier to see turning points and discern a hinge than in some other books. For example, since books like Psalms and Proverbs are collections of writings, the books themselves won't have a hinge. Instead, consider each chapter individually and look for turning points that help unveil the chapter's main message.

In the epistles, we're not looking for action but teaching direction. The author often turns the reader from *learning* to *doing*—from *indicative* (statements of teaching: This is what God has done for you) to *imperatives* (commands of response: This is what it looks like to live out the teaching). The indicatives reveal the epistles' heartbeat. The imperatives direct the people's hands and feet.

Today's passage contains the hinge in the gospel of Mark—the moment Jesus drastically changed the direction of His ministry from His miracles to His crucifixion and resurrection.

PRACTICE SESSION: MARK 8:22–38

INTENT

- From the moment Jesus began His public ministry, He demonstrated spiritual truths by His works. The moment He called His twelve disciples to follow Him, He continually taught them through both *show* and *tell*—through His works and words.
- Herod feared Jesus was John the Baptist resurrected (Mark 6:14).
- Malachi prophesied Elijah would return before the coming of the Lord (Malachi 4:5).
- God promised to raise up another prophet like Moses (Deuteronomy 18:18).
- Jesus's claim to be the "Son of God" wasn't a claim to be "from God" or to be a "servant of God" but to be God Himself (John 5:18).

TRUTH

Pray and read Mark 8:22–38. As we enter this scene, remember the context immediately before this passage when Jesus asked His disciples if they have eyes but cannot see (Mark 8:18). Jesus's disciples were still struggling to see the truth about Him. As you read today's passage, listen carefully to Christ's words as He heals the blind man. Watch our omnipotent Lord's every action. Take notes on what He and the blind man say and do. Then listen in as Jesus asks His disciples the big question.

I'll start.

TRIUNE GOD	OTHERS
JESUS	**BLIND MAN**
• Leads blind man by hand (*He's compassionate and intentional*) • Spits on man's eyes/ touches his eyes (*gives vivid demonstration the blind man can understand*)	• Friends display faith in Jesus. Bring blind man to Him, beg Him to touch blind man (*Why "touch"? Why not "heal"?*)
	PETER
	DISCIPLES

DAY FIVE | 115

- Based on all we've read so far in Mark and in the context of this passage, which verse do you think is the hinge of Mark?

- Despite Jesus not coming to earth in glory like a conquering warrior as the Jews expected of the Messiah, Peter sees who Jesus is—the promised one, the Christ. How have you come to understand Jesus differently than when you first trusted in Him? Did you expect Him to rush in and fix all your trials? Did you think you'd be free from suffering? Compare what you first imagined or believed with what Scripture reveals about Him.

TRANSFORMATION

God gave Peter spiritual sight to see who Jesus is, but Peter's "vision" was more like seeing trees walking. He saw who Jesus is—His divine nature as the true Son of God. Now Peter and the other disciples need to see the other side of the hinge—what Jesus will do for their salvation.

Mark 8:29 is the hinge that turns the page from Jesus's performing miracles that reveal His divine *identity* as the Son of God to Jesus's dying and rising to life, which reveals His divine *ministry* as the one true Savior of the world.

The hinge in a Christian's life is the moment we receive spiritual life and believe in Jesus for salvation. When Christ enters a life, He flips the script. We were dead in our sins, but through salvation, Christ makes us alive in Him. There's no greater change a soul can experience than receiving spiritual life.

After salvation, the power of the Holy Spirit begins our lifelong journey of being transformed day by day into more and more Christlikeness (Romans 8:29). For some, transformation begins like a lightning bolt—an addict released immediately from a years-long dependency. Other times, we transform more gradually as God's Word changes our thinking and habits.

One day, we'll witness the turning point all creation longs to see—Christ's return. In that day, nothing will ever be the same again. Every knee will bow in heaven and on earth and under the earth, and every tongue will confess that Jesus Christ is Lord—He is Yahweh—all to the glory of God (Philippians 2:10–11). And we who belong to Christ will worship Him as we've never worshiped before.

TRANSFORMATIONAL TRUTH

When Christ enters a life, He flips the script.

Add to or review your Attributes of God list at the back of the book.

How is Jesus calling you to respond to today's passage? What will it look like in your life to have the script of your life flipped from death to life? To pick up your cross and follow Him? Journal your response.

_____
_____
_____
_____
_____
_____
_____
_____
_____
_____

TRANSFORMATIONAL BIBLE STUDY PRINCIPLES

- ✓ Turning points in the Bible emphasize spiritual truths and move the reader to specific Christlike responses.
- ✓ In narratives, we look for a change in action. In epistles, we look for a change in teaching from what Christ has done to how we're to respond.

MEMORY VERSE: PSALM 119:18

Write out this week's memory verse.

WEEK FOUR

Ears to *Hear*

MARK 9:1–10:52

This is my beloved Son; listen to him.
—Mark 9:7

WEEK FOUR — day one

God's Unfolding Plan

TODAY'S READING

Mark 9:1–13

"When you write," I asked a novelist friend, "do you know the end of the story from the beginning?"

"Not really," she said. "I have a basic idea, but I discovered that if the writer isn't surprised by the ending, the reader won't be either."

My friend's writing plan excites me as I wait for her next novel, but it would terrify me if this was how God wrote our story.

THE INTERDEPENDENCY OF THE OLD AND NEW TESTAMENTS

The old adage "Out with the old and in with the new!" doesn't work with the Old and New Testaments. If we toss out either, we've lost the fullness of the story. We're left with only partial understanding. God structured His Word to be interdependent—each Testament explains the other. The Old and New bring aha! clarity to each other and to our understanding of the whole Bible and the full counsel of God's will, purposes, and plans.

Over thousands of years, through the pens and styluses of His authors, God unfolded His revelation of Himself and His eternal plan of salvation bit by bit. God directed each word to unfold a little more of His revelation at the right time.

The Old Testament prophets wrote of the Messiah's coming, but God's New Testament people didn't recognize His arrival. His coming didn't match what they expected. They didn't realize until after He came that the prophets had written not of one glorious coming but of two—first as the Suffering Son and Servant and then as the conquering King and Lord of all.

PUTTING THE PUZZLE PIECES TOGETHER

Whenever someone first reads the whole Bible, they'll likely feel lost in sections; it's like putting a puzzle together without the picture on the box. Jesus is the picture. With continued study and time, the puzzle of the Bible comes together in our minds, and God's unfolding story and picture of Christ rises clearer off Scripture's pages.

We can't put the whole picture of any book of the Bible together without pieces from both Testaments. Mark's gospel tells a complete and glorious story, but it's only when we fit it together with events from the Old Testament that we can truly understand it.

The story of Israel's exodus out of Egypt makes spiritual truths we would have missed pop off Mark's pages. Fit into this understanding the stories of God's work in His people in the wilderness and the promised land, and our understanding, and thus our faith, increases all the more.

With each new piece of the Bible that we fit into our understanding of Scripture, the fuller our understanding grows of God's revelation of Himself and His plans. We see Jesus more clearly, become better prepared for His return and eternal kingdom, and solidify our faith so it grows more unshakeable.

In today's passage, God stunned Peter, James, and John when He brought the Old Testament into their New Testament world in technicolor glory.

PRACTICE SESSION: MARK 9:1–13

INTENT

Views differ about what event Jesus refers to in Mark 9:1. When we look at the context of the adjacent verses, it seems clear Jesus is speaking of when Peter, James, and John get a glimpse of the coming of God's kingdom in power through Jesus's transfiguration.

TRUTH

Read Mark 1:2–13. Imagine walking up the high mountain with Jesus, Peter, James, and John. Feel awe-tinged fear as Jesus radiates with light and Elijah and Moses suddenly appear. Hear—and listen—as God speak from the cloud. Remember the Truth questions as you make notes. I'll start.

TRIUNE GOD	OTHERS
FATHER	**ELIJAH & MOSES**
	• Talk with Jesus (*What did they talk about?*)
JESUS	**DISCIPLES**
• Transfigured "Changed in form" • BRIGHT w/ glory • Fulfills Mark 9:1 • Displays Mark 1:15, "the Kingdom of God is near" • *Transfiguration reminds me of OT events*	• Peter, James, and John go with Jesus up high mountain

DAY ONE

- How do the following passages help you better understand Mark 9:1–13?

    Exodus 24:15–16: _____

    _____

    Malachi 4:4–5: _____

    _____

    Luke 9:31: _____

    _____

    Revelation 1:12–19: _____

    _____

- Write out what God said in Mark 9:7 and list various ways we might best respond to this command today. _____

    _____

    _____

    _____

    _____

TRANSFORMATION

After the Exodus from Egypt, God spoke to the Israelites from Mount Sinai. God's voice struck the people with such awe and fear that they begged Moses, "You speak to us, and we will listen; but do not let God speak to us, lest we die" (Exodus 20:18–19). Eventually, though, their fear faded as the sound of His voice faded from their conscience. So later, when Moses met with God on the top of Mount Sinai for forty days, God's people created a statue of a golden calf to worship (Exodus 32).

Living on this side of the cross, we have the great benefit of reading not only God's words from Mount Sinai and Israel's entire exodus, as well as centuries later on the Mount of Transfiguration, but also the rest of Jesus's words recorded in Matthew, Mark, Luke, and John—and all sixty-six books of the Bible.

As we study the whole Bible, God's Spirit will open our eyes to greater and greater understanding of His unfolding revelation of redemption. Hear the Father speak through His Word, listen to His Son call you to Himself, and faithfully follow Him by His Spirit's power.

When Christ finally returns and we see the end of the story and fulfillment of all His Word, everything will happen exactly as He planned. There'll be no surprises for the Author. We, however, will be amazed, for "no eye has seen, nor ear heard, nor the heart of man imagined, what God has prepared for those who love him" (1 Corinthians 2:9).

TRANSFORMATIONAL TRUTH

Listen to Jesus from Genesis to Revelation. Follow Him from the cross to radiant glory.

Add to or review your Attributes of God list at the back of the book.

If you truly believe what God's Word reveals about His glorious works in the past and His promises for the future, how will you live differently today and tomorrow? What truths will you remember in the valleys and proclaim on the mountains? Journal your response.

_____

_____

_____

_____

_____

TRANSFORMATIONAL BIBLE STUDY PRINCIPLES

- ✓ God structured His Word to be interdependent—each Testament explains the other.
- ✓ The Old and New bring aha! clarity to each other and to our understanding of the whole Bible and the full counsel of God's will, purposes, and plans.

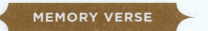

Write out this week's memory verse and read it aloud five times.

This is my beloved Son; listen to him. (Mark 9:7)

WEEK FOUR — day two

Pray

TODAY'S READING

Mark 9:14–29

I feel the disciples' pain.

I've never been able to whistle like my sister, but I could whistle a pretty good tune. But no more. Melissa's whistle could raise Lazarus from the grave. Mine couldn't call a dog that's sitting on my lap.

I'm not comparing my surprising loss of whistle powers to the disciples' loss of being able to cast out demons. I'm just saying I understand their confusion. How did I lose this skill? How could I suddenly not be able to do today what I could do yesterday?

NEVER FORGET TO REMEMBER TO PRAY

Of all the skills we learn and forget, prayer should never make this list. Prayer isn't like water wings or arm floaties. It's not something we use until we know how to swim on our own. Effective prayer acknowledges we could never swim at all without God's power. It says, "I can't, Father, but you can." Prayer is the natural outpouring of this acknowledgment.

Effective prayer doesn't pray for more faith in our ability to do what God calls us to do. It prays for more faith in the One who calls us and is faithful. He will do it (1 Thessalonians 5:24).

The difference between effective and ineffective prayer is the faith with which it's prayed. Faith placed in Christ has power. All other faith sinks us.

Let's guard ourselves from ever thinking, whether in life or in Bible study, that we're so teamed up with the Lord that we can now swim on our own—or swim off "in His name." Because, as He told His apostles, "apart from me you can do nothing" (John 15:5).

PRACTICE SESSION: MARK 9:14–29

INTENT

- The boy's seizures resemble epilepsy, but Jesus cast out a demon; he didn't heal a disease.
- The phrase "and fasting" in Mark 9:29, seen in older translations such as the King James Version, was likely added later.

TRUTH

Pray and read Mark 9:14–29. Imagine you're one of the disciples surrounded by the arguing crowd. Feel your shock and disappointment when you fail to cast out a demon from a boy. Feel the dad's despair. When Jesus walks up with Peter, James, and John, feel your relief at His appearance and shame at His rebuke. Make notes in the chart to help you draw out the message Mark wants us to understand. I'll start.

TRIUNE GOD	OTHERS
JESUS	**DISCIPLES**
<ul><li>Asked what they're arguing about (*He's not curious; He's bringing the problem to light*)</li><li>Rebukes disciples and scribes. Calls them a "faithless generation." (*Jesus never insults; He convicts and rebukes*)</li><li>Reveals true problem: _____</li></ul>	<ul><li>***Problem:*** Can't cast out demon. *Why?*</li><li>Called a "faithless generation"</li><li>***True problem:*** unbelief, not inability</li></ul>
	CROWD/SCRIBES
	<ul><li>***Scribes:*** arguing (*as always*)</li><li>***Crowd:*** "greatly amazed" by Jesus (*Did His face glow with glory remnants?*)</li><li>Called a "faithless generation"</li></ul>
	BOY'S FATHER
	<ul><li>Problem: Son has a demon (*his seeking displays faith in Jesus's power to heal*)</li></ul>
	DEMON
	<ul><li>Tortures boy</li><li>Makes boy deaf and unable to speak</li><li>Freaks out when sees Jesus</li><li>Tries to destroy boy (*God alone determines the day of our death*)</li></ul>

- Jesus says the disciples couldn't cast out the demon because they didn't pray. Who is the one person who prayed in today's passage?

- What did he pray?

- Everything in today's passage builds up to and from the father's prayer—a prayer about belief, not healing. Jesus rebuked the disciples, crowd, and dad about belief, not effort. Belief in what? Or rather, belief in whom?

- How does Jesus's rebuke and the father's prayer challenge, convict, and/or encourage you?

- Part of the indispensable armor of God is prayer. How should we pray? See Ephesians 6:18 and 1 Thessalonians 5:17.

TRANSFORMATION

I've never prayed for the Lord to restore my whistle. I'm fine without whistle skills. The disciples' failure, though, meant the boy must continue to suffer the demon's torture and attempted destruction. The disciples had enjoyed great success before, but no longer. Somewhere along the way they stopped praying. They began to rely on their own strength, as if the authority to cast out demons originated from themselves rather than from Christ and His authority.

It's easier than we realize to slip unaware from a prayer-dependent and Holy Spirit–led life into self-dependency and the sin of unbelief in God's Word, which is rooted in pride.

Like Peter, Christians can fluctuate between belief and unbelief. I'm not talking about belief for salvation; I'm talking about belief *after* salvation. Peter confessed Jesus as the Christ and then a moment later rebuked Jesus (Mark 8:29–33).

When we say we believe Jesus does all things well, but we pray like we're His needed and wiser advisor, our prayer exposes our prideful unbelief.

When we say we believe Jesus is always good and sovereign over all things, but we wring our hands and lose sleep over our trials, our anxiety exposes an area of unbelief.

Just as Jesus called the disciples to more faithful prayer, so He calls us. Let's pray for more belief.

Just as Jesus called the boy's father to faith in Him, so He calls us to greater faith in Him alone. Let's answer Jesus's call with the father's honest prayer: "Lord, I believe. Help my unbelief."

TRANSFORMATIONAL TRUTH

Effective prayer says, "I can't, Father, but you can. Lord, I believe. Help my unbelief."

Add to or review your Attributes of God list at the back of the book.

If you truly believe what God has revealed through today's passage, how will your prayer life change? What will it look like in your daily life? Journal your response.

_____
_____
_____
_____
_____
_____
_____
_____
_____
_____
_____

TRANSFORMATIONAL BIBLE STUDY PRINCIPLES

- ✓ It's easier than we realize to slip unaware from a prayer-dependent and Holy Spirit–led life into self-dependency.
- ✓ Effective prayer prays for more faith in the One who calls us and is faithful. He will do it.

MEMORY VERSE: MARK 9:7

Write out this week's memory verse.

WEEK FOUR — *day three*

Poetry

TODAY'S READING

Mark 9:30–50

My ideas always seemed to exceed our bank account, and my emotions exceeded my wisdom and restraint. Will my kind husband's patience last? Will he eventually regret marrying someone he continually has to rein in?

When I poured out my fears to Larry, he smiled. "We're a good team," he said. "I keep your feet on the ground, and you keep my head in the clouds."

I doubt Larry knew the lasting power his words would hold—his most comforting and memorable words. He knows now.

THE POWER OF POETRY

You might not think my husband is a poet. I'm sure he doesn't know it. (You're groaning, but I had to say it.) English poetry tends toward rhyme (sometimes terrible rhyme), but not Hebrew poetry. The ancient poets created non-rhyming images we could see and feel through beautiful and vivid expressions. They often coupled these images with parallel lines for emphasis or to lead us to compare and contrast the images and awaken a lasting understanding.

Poetry fills more lines in the Bible than any other biblical genre except narrative. If you're not a poetry lover, be encouraged. Hebrew poetry is not "Roses are red, violets are blue." Nor is it the dark rantings of a tortured poet in a smoky lounge.

The Bible's poetry is like the gentle cadence of ocean waves that mesmerize and draw us in, and the crackle of fireworks that ignite our senses—like Larry's words to me. One poetic line packed with meaning makes us ponder truth we might have quickly forgotten but will now remember forever. Can you finish this line?

"The LORD is my shepherd. _____."

FOUR TIPS FOR UNDERSTANDING BIBLICAL POETRY

The following four methods can lead us to the meaning of the poetic message.[10] Not every poetic verse or passage needs every method. Use only those that are relevant to the passage you're studying.

1. Experience the image.

> Ask: *What image has the author created?*

> The authors put flesh on ideas and concepts. They make the abstract concrete to help us understand the message.

2. Recognize the relationship.

> Ask: *What's the connection between the concrete image and the abstract truth?*

> The relationship between the concrete image and the abstract truth is key to recognizing the meat of the message.

3. Feel the emotion.

> Ask: *What emotion does the image evoke?*

> The authors create particular images to evoke specific emotions because these emotions lead us to the spiritual truth and message. Feel the emotion.

4. Follow the logic.

> Ask: *What's the most logical path this image takes me on?*

> Emotion alone can lead us to illogical and even dangerous conclusions. The Holy Spirit inspired each emotion-evoking image to lead us on a logical path to a divine conclusion—to the spiritual truth God wants us to know, believe, and obey.

POETIC TECHNIQUES

Authors choose the poetic techniques that best convey their message. The list of techniques in the Bible is too long for this lesson. Here are some of the most common:

Metaphors compare two dissimilar objects using forms of the verb "to be."
"We are the clay, and you are our potter." (Isaiah 64:8)

Similes compare two dissimilar objects using the words "like" or "as."
"His face was like the sun shining in full strength." (Revelation 1:16)

Hyperboles are deliberate exaggeration for emphasis.
"If your hand causes you to sin, cut it off." (Mark 9:43)

Paradoxes are ridiculous or contradictory statements designed to make a point.
"If anyone would be first, he must be last of all and servant of all." (Mark 9:35)

Parallelism uses the repetition of similar or opposite words, thoughts, or ideas or the repetition of sounds to emphasize and lead to the spiritual truth.
"Having eyes do you not see, and having ears do you not hear?" (Mark 8:18)

PRACTICE SESSION: MARK 9:30–50

Consider the four techniques for understanding poetry as you read today's passage and interpret the poetic and figurative language. I'll start.

"If anyone would be first, he must be last of all and servant of all" (Mark 9:35).

1. Experience the image.

Jesus created a *paradox* of two contrasting images.
"First"—Someone of highest position and honor, as a king before whom everyone bows and runs to obey.

DAY THREE | 135

"Servant"—A person of least honor, who runs to perform the commands of their master no matter how undesirable the task.

2. Recognize the relationship.

The *first* and *servant* are opposites.

3. Feel the emotion.

In the culture of their day, the original listeners would have felt shock over Jesus's statement, maybe even horror, that anyone could be *first* by degrading themselves and positioning themselves as the lowest of servants.

4. Follow the logic.

Earthly kings don't perform others' menial tasks, but the logic of Jesus's paradox leads us to the conclusion that in God's kingdom, those who run to serve even the least of society will be first in His kingdom. They'll be like King Jesus, who came not to be served but to serve to the point of willingly going to the cross to give His life as a ransom for us (Mark 10:45).

- Work through these same four steps as you study the following verses in today's passage.

    verse 37—parallelism

    _____
    _____
    _____
    _____

    verse 40—paradox

    _____
    _____
    _____

verses 42–47—hyperbole

_____
_____
_____
_____

TRANSFORMATION

Larry keeps my feet on the ground, but he also keeps my head in the clouds with his sense of humor, kindness, and love. Even greater, Jesus grounds our feet in the truth and sends our hearts and minds into the heights of heaven with His gospel of grace, mercy, and love. Jesus is our perfect Servant-King.

> For even the Son of Man came not to be served but to serve, and to give his life as a ransom for many. (Mark 10:45)

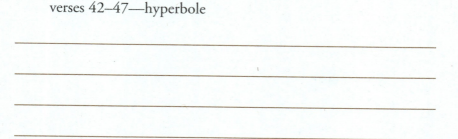

TRANSFORMATIONAL TRUTH

Jesus grounds our feet in the truth, and His gospel of grace, mercy, and love sends our hearts and minds into the heights of heaven.

Add to or review your Attributes of God list at the back of the book.

If you really believe Christ's words in today's passage, what will it look like in your life? How will it affect the decisions you make? How will it change who and how you serve others? Journal your response.

_____
_____
_____
_____
_____
_____
_____
_____
_____
_____

TRANSFORMATIONAL BIBLE STUDY PRINCIPLES
- ✓ Poetry brings a message to life in memorable and often vivid words and images.
- ✓ To interpret poetic passages, we want to experience the image, recognize the relationship, feel the emotion, and follow the logic.

> **MEMORY VERSE: MARK 9:7**

Write out this week's memory verse.

WEEK FOUR — *day four*

Narrative and Law

TODAY'S READING
Mark 10:1–31

Once upon an always, there was, is, and forever will be our loving, gracious, and holy Savior. His story is the greatest ever told.

THE POWER OF STORY AND GOD'S LAW OF LOVE

The power of story comes from its ability to make us feel emotions and form lifelike connections with the characters.

"Whoever divorces his wife and marries another commits adultery against her" (Mark 10:11). Can you sense the sting of betrayal and abandonment?

"Go, sell all that you have and give to the poor, and you will have treasure in heaven; and come, follow me" (v. 21). Does your stomach sink from the pull of earthly treasures despite heaven's promises?

"With man it is impossible, but not with God. For all things are possible with God" (v. 27). Do your shoulders relax and your heart lighten with the impossible made gloriously certain?

The stories these verses tell fill us with emotions.

Law fills us with emotions, too.

Sometimes we feel relief. *No one is allowed to hurt me.*

Other times we're afraid. *I'm in trouble now.*

Or annoyed. *Don't tell me what to do.*

Our problem with law isn't the law. Our problem is with our heart—it's impossibly emotional, fickle, and ruled by sin. But Christ is our certain cure. That is the story of the law of love the Bible tells—the overwhelming story of our salvation that though God's law condemns us, Christ's love saves us.

HOW TO UNDERSTAND NARRATIVE

Narrative is the genre of storytelling. When we study narrative, we immerse ourselves in the characters, setting, and plot with its rising *conflict*, *climax*, and *resolution*. The more we live the story (at least in our imagination), the more we understand it and its main point or theme.

Narratives are typically literal, not figurative. They mean what they say and say what they mean. The context reveals whether the author is using literal or figurative language.

HOW TO UNDERSTAND THE LAW GENRE

In order to understand the law genre, it's vital that we grasp the twofold overarching purpose of the Mosaic law.

> *So then, the law was our guardian until Christ came, in order that we might be justified by faith. (Galatians 3:24)*

1. **Tutor.** The law awakened Israel's awareness of sin. They needed to learn they could never perfectly keep the law and thus needed a Savior. Their continual failure to keep the law proved their need. (We also prove our need.)
2. **Guardian.** The original word for *guardian* in the Greek referred to a tutor who was tasked with training the son in more than reading, writing, and arithmetic. He also educated him in life and ethics.[11] The law kept God's people safe, trained them in the truth, and pointed them to Christ.

In the Old Testament, God established laws (statutes) and covenants (promises). Most of God's laws were conditional, as in "If you do this, then I will do that." Some divide the Mosaic law into three categories:

1. The **moral law** encompassed God's justice and judgment; think Ten Commandments (Exodus 20).
2. The **ceremonial law** regulated how the people could come to God to worship Him for His great works and to find forgiveness without being obliterated because of their sin.
3. The **civil law** directed the rulers and judges in how to govern God's people.

As we study God's unconditional covenants with Abraham and David ("Because I am God, I will . . .") and His conditional Mosaic law and covenants ("If you do . . . then I will . . ."), we gain a greater understanding of God and of this great salvation we've received.

God never told stories for sheer entertainment or solely for historical record but to reveal spiritual truth. In today's passage, Christ uses the power of narrative and the law to spotlight important truths about God's kingdom.

PRACTICE SESSION: MARK 10:1–31

INTENT

- In Deuteronomy 24:1–4, Moses created a hypothetical legal case about divorce with a "When this happens . . ." statement. Moses never condoned the hypothetical husband's behavior. He simply stated the case and gave the law, which was designed to protect a wife from her husband's sinful whims. Israel's religious leaders expanded this law. They made it acceptable for a husband to divorce his wife for displeasing him in any way, such as burning dinner or not looking as pretty as the cutie next door.[12]
- Children didn't have rights in ancient Israel. They were considered insignificant.
- When Jesus talked about a camel passing through the eye of a needle, He used exaggeration to emphasize the impossible.

TRUTH

Pray and read Mark 10:1–31. Enter the scene and feel the characters' emotions. Notice how they use the law and the power of story to elicit the desired response. Remember the Truth questions as you make notes in the T-chart.

TRIUNE GOD	OTHERS

- The Pharisees misrepresent God's character (vv. 1–12). The disciples (vv. 13–16) and most likely the rich young ruler (vv. 17–22) misunderstand God's character. Their response to God's law and love exposes the true condition of their hearts. What does Jesus reveal about each heart?

Pharisees:

_____

_____

Disciples:

_____

_____

Rich young ruler:

_____

_____

- When will all who trust in Jesus enjoy the rewards of faith and obedience (see vv. 29–31)? How does this both encourage and sober you today and as you look to the future?

_____

_____

_____

TRANSFORMATION

In perfect love Christ gave His life on the cross to purchase the freedom of His bride, the church. He satisfies our deepest desires, lifts the last to first, and makes us His beloved bride.

TRANSFORMATIONAL TRUTH

**Once upon an always,
there was, is, and forever will be
our loving, gracious, and holy Savior.**

Add to or review your Attributes of God list at the back of the book.

If you truly believe what Christ revealed through today's passage, how will you respond? What will you stop loving more than God? What will it look like for you to "leave everything" to follow your loving, gracious, and holy Savior? Journal your response.

_____

_____

_____

_____
_____
_____
_____
_____
_____
_____
_____

TRANSFORMATIONAL BIBLE STUDY PRINCIPLES

- ✓ When you study the narrative genre, immerse yourself in the characters, setting, and plot with its rising conflict, climax, and resolution.
- ✓ When you study the law genre, remember God designed all His covenants and commands (the ceremonial, moral, and civil laws) to teach us about Christ and drive us to Him.

MEMORY VERSE: MARK 9:7

Write out this week's memory verse.

WEEK FOUR — day five

Questions

TODAY'S READING

Mark 10:32–52

Do you know who asked the first question in the Bible?

The serpent. He asked Eve, "Did God actually say, 'You shall not eat of any tree in the garden'?" (Genesis 3:1).

The Bible's first recorded question was the evil planting of a seed of doubt about God.

The next question was the Lord calling to His fallen children: "Where are you?" (v. 9).

Between the moment Adam and Eve rebelled and God proclaimed the gospel in Genesis 3:15, every sentence God spoke was a question. The question we might ask now is why an all-knowing God would ever need to ask a question.

GOD'S PERFECT QUESTIONS

I know I'm stating the obvious, but God is not like us. He never needs new information. He's not even curious because He knows everything. He's intentional in all He does, including asking questions—rhetorical and direct questions like, "What do you want me to do for you?"

Whenever we come across one of God's questions, stop and study it. What does His question reveal about Himself or about the person He's questioning? What does He want them (and us) to realize, confess, or ponder?

Jesus asked around sixty questions in Mark,[13] including one of my favorites in the Bible: "Who do you say that I am?" (Mark 8:29). Peter nailed the answer: "You are the Christ." But he still had much to learn about our Lord, as did James and John and the rest of Jesus's disciples—and us. In today's passage, Jesus asks one question twice. Why twice? Let's find out.

PRACTICE SESSION: MARK 10:32–52

INTENT

- Jesus's detailed prophecy of His death and resurrection contradicted everything the Jews believed about the coming of the Messiah and His kingdom, such as the Messiah cannot die, and no one can bring themselves back from the dead.
- The Jews expected the Messiah to come for war against His enemies, and the enemy at that time was Rome.
- The disciples assumed those closest to the Messiah would receive honored positions in His kingdom.
- The cup in the Old Testament often symbolized suffering or divine judgment (see Jeremiah 25:15).
- "Baptism" could remind the disciples of John's baptism for the repentance of sin, of Jesus's baptism by John, and of the picture of being fully immersed.
- Son of David and Son of Man were Old Testament titles for the Messiah (2 Samuel 7:12–16; Daniel 7:13).

TRUTH

Pray and read Mark 10:32–52. Follow Jesus to Jerusalem and listen to Him share the horrid future awaiting Him there. Walk in James's and John's shoes and hear Jesus's unexpected answer; sit in the place of blind, begging Bartimaeus; and ponder Jesus's twice-repeated question (vv. 36, 51). Remember the Truth questions as you make notes.

TRIUNE GOD	OTHERS
	JAMES AND JOHN
	BARTIMAEUS

- Write out Jesus's repeated question in verses 36 and 51.

- What does James and John's bold request reveal about their hearts—both good and bad?

- How does Jesus respond to the brothers' request?

- Why do you think the disciples were upset with James and John?

_____

_____

While Mark doesn't say why the disciples were indignant with the brothers, Jesus's ensuing teaching seems to indicate all the disciples wanted the highest positions for themselves.

Christ's question to the brothers leads to the heartbeat of the gospel of Mark.

- Write out Mark 10:45.

_____

_____

_____

Most scholars consider this verse the climax and the lens through which we can understand all of Mark. It's not the hinge verse when everything changed, but rather the heartbeat of the gospel of Mark.

Immediately after this verse we meet a poor, blind Bartimaeus.

- How does Jesus respond to Bartimaeus?

_____

_____

In today's passage, Jesus asks one question twice and exposes two different desires. Bartimaeus wants to see; James and John want the highest seats of honor and glory. Jesus wants to give all three of these men both sight and honor and glory.

Jesus gave Bartimaeus physical *and* spiritual sight—and honor and glory as he entered God's kingdom by faith.

Jesus gave James and John increasing spiritual sight and ultimate honor and glory as they picked up their crosses and faithfully followed Him.

What is your cry? What do you want Jesus to do for you?

TRANSFORMATION

In the final book of the Bible, Jesus never asked any questions. Perhaps the first of only six questions in Revelation explains why.

> I saw a mighty angel proclaiming with a loud voice, "Who is worthy to open the scroll and break its seals?" (Revelation 5:2)

Jesus is the answer to the question. He is worthy.

> Worthy are you to take the scroll
>   and to open its seals,
> for you were slain, and by your blood you ransomed
>   people for God
>   from every tribe and language and people and
>   nation,
> and you have made them a kingdom and priests to
>   our God,
>   and they shall reign on the earth.
>   (Revelation 5:9–10)

If Jesus asked me, "What do you want me to do for you?" after studying today's passage, all I can answer is, "Jesus, you have given me everything. What could I ask for myself but to let me serve you. But if I may ask for my loved ones, Jesus, I ask you to save them as you have saved me. I can't. But you can."

TRANSFORMATIONAL TRUTH

Every need of the heart, every longing of the soul, finds its fulfillment in Jesus.

Add to or review your Attributes of God list at the back of the book.

If you truly believe what God has revealed in today's passage, how will you answer Jesus's question? What do you want Him to do for you? What request would you make? Journal your response.

TRANSFORMATIONAL BIBLE STUDY PRINCIPLES

- ✓ God never asks questions for His benefit. He already knows everything.
- ✓ Whenever you come across one of God's questions, stop and study it. Consider what His question reveals about Himself or about the person He's questioning. What does He want them—and us—to realize, confess, or ponder?

MEMORY VERSE: MARK 9:7

Write out this week's memory verse.

WEEK FIVE

Behold Your *King!*

MARK 11:1–13:37

The fear of the Lord is the beginning of wisdom,
and the knowledge of the Holy One is insight.
—Proverbs 9:10

WEEK FIVE — day one

Behold Your King!

TODAY'S READING

Mark 11:1–11

"I don't love the Bible," Sarah admitted to her pastor.

"Read all of it," he said.

She did. She still didn't love it.

"This time," he said, "read it to know who God is."

She was halfway into the Old Testament when she fell in love with the Bible—and God.

As Sarah told her story, I wanted to shout, "Yes!" because her story was so much like mine.

Like Sarah, I'd never read all of the Bible, but even more than wanting to love God's Word, I longed for the abiding peace and joy the Bible promises. They eluded me. Maybe being a "good Christian" was for other people. For better people. Despite all my efforts, I could still out-temper-tantrum a toddler over the most trivial disappointments.

My Christian life had become an exhausting life of one step forward, two stumbles back.

By God's grace, I had an idea. I reached for my Bible. Maybe what I was missing rested on one of the many pages I'd never read. I determined I'd read every page, not to know how to be a better Christian, but only to know who God is. To know Him.

Early the next morning when only the sun and I were awake, I opened my Bible to Genesis 1:1 and whispered a desperate prayer. "Show me you, God, on every page. I just want to know you."

IT'S ALL ABOUT HIM!

I know I've said this before, but we can't say it enough: the Bible is all about Christ and His salvation. Possibly the most important principle we'll ever learn for studying the Bible is to behold our King. To keep our eyes on the Lord.

If we truly behold Christ in His Word with eyes of faith, we'll follow Him and His commands with more and more of our heart, soul, mind, and strength. Our lives will be a rewarding adventure with our Lord, regardless of the many trials we'll endure. Eternal rewards wait for us in heaven—rewards beyond anything our minds could imagine on earth.

In today's passage, we'll join in the celebration of Christ, and we'll sharpen this most vital Bible study principle: Behold your King!

PRACTICE SESSION: MARK 11:1–11

INTENT

- In the ancient Near East, horses were for war. A king rode on a donkey when he came in peace.
- Unbroken donkeys don't let you ride them.
- The ancients threw clothes on the road for their king to walk on as a way of honoring him (2 Kings 9:13). They waved palm branches to celebrate their king's victories.
- The people welcomed Christ with words from Psalm 118:19–29. Psalms 113–118 are known as the *Hallel*, which means "praise." God's people sang these six Hallel psalms to celebrate Passover.
- *Hosanna* means "Save, we pray."
- Before Christ, the only place to find salvation for sin was the temple.

TRUTH

Pray and read Mark 11:1–11. Behold your King as He rides into Jerusalem on a donkey's colt. He's performed amazing miracles among thousands, but He's never entered a city like a king. Hear the crowds hail Christ. Feel the breeze from the waving palm branches and sense the people's adoration. Notice everything.

Today, we'll focus only on Jesus. We'll behold our King. On the T-chart, note what Mark reveals about our Lord, and fill in parallel truths from the context of the whole Bible as you're able. I'll start.

TRIUNE GOD
JESUS
Jesus's power is sovereign. • He empowered His disciples to follow and execute His will exactly as He'd planned. • He prepared a donkey's colt to ride and prepared the heart of the owner to surrender it to Jesus's disciples. Jesus's creation knows Him. • This untrained, unbroken donkey let Jesus ride him. It trusted its Creator—Jesus. Jesus is worthy of all worship and will receive the worship due His name according to His purposes and will. • The people spread their cloaks in the road for Jesus to walk on. • They cut palm branches and waved them and hailed Jesus as their King. • Jesus didn't need the rocks to cry out because the people did (Luke 19:40).

Read Zechariah 9:9 aloud and picture today's passage as you read.

- Luke recorded how the Pharisees opposed Jesus when He entered Jerusalem and how Jesus wept over Jerusalem (Luke 19:39–44). Mark left these out. Instead, what spiritual truths does Mark focus on?

_____

_____

_____

TRANSFORMATION

When I read through the whole Bible for the first time, studying the Bible became refreshing almost overnight because I finally took my eyes completely off myself and off what I "have to do." Instead, I fixed my eyes on God and His matchless character. I discovered how little I had known about who God truly is. As I looked at His character, nature, and ways on every page, I beheld my King and marveled—and was transformed.

The Jews thought they knew what their Messiah would be like when He came—a warrior who'd destroy their political enemies.

The Gentiles thought they knew how to find salvation—by pleasing their myriad of false gods.

How easy it is for us to make God into a king of our own imagination. We envision Him as a king who'd never allow His children to suffer or ask us to forsake our dreams for His will—as if His will is bad. Or we imagine Him as a severe God who's never truly pleased with us.

No wonder so many of us are like unbroken donkeys who don't fully trust their Creator. The God we've created in our minds looks a lot like us. But if we come to God's Word and truly behold our King, we'll see Him as He truly is—and we'll be like Jesus's trusting colt. We'll yield to Him and trust Him.

When we truly behold our King, abiding peace and joy will rule our hearts and minds.

TRANSFORMATIONAL TRUTH

When we behold our King, our King's glory holds our hearts.

Add to or review your Attributes of God list at the back of the book.

If you truly believe Christ as He's revealed Himself in today's passage, how will your desires and attitudes change? What will it look like in your life to continually behold your King? Journal your response.

TRANSFORMATIONAL BIBLE STUDY PRINCIPLES

- ✓ Possibly the most important principle we'll ever learn for studying the Bible is to behold our King.
- ✓ The Bible is all about Christ and His salvation.

MEMORY VERSE

Write out this week's memory verse and read it aloud five times.

The fear of the LORD is the beginning of wisdom, and the knowledge of the Holy One is insight.
(Proverbs 9:10)

WEEK FIVE — day two

Types, Patterns, Illustrations

TODAY'S READING
Mark 11:12–12:12

"Is he as kind as he looks?" Mom asked. She took the photo from my hand and adjusted her glasses for a closer look at my new boyfriend.

"He's even kinder," I said.

She smiled.

I married him.

SNAPSHOTS

The Bible is a verbal and visual masterpiece. After God spoke the gospel to Adam and Eve, He gave them a snapshot of the gospel. He took an innocent animal (could it have been a lamb?) and clothed Adam and Eve in its skin as a picture of the garments of salvation and a robe of Christ's righteousness (Isaiah 61:10).

In Romans 5:14, God declared Adam a *type* of Jesus Christ (or, depending on your Bible translation, a pattern, symbol, representation, figure, or prototype).

Throughout the Bible, God created vivid snapshots that displayed spiritual truths, particularly about Christ and His kingdom. Old Testament individuals such as Adam, and objects such as the temple, and every aspect of the sacrificial system foreshadowed New Testament fulfillments of Christ.

God wove *themes* such as creation, redemption, and exile from Genesis to Revelation.

Patterns such as Christ, the apostles, and Israel give us examples to follow or not follow. (Let's follow Christ's and the apostles' examples; not Israel's when they rebelled in the wilderness.)

> Beginning with Moses and all the Prophets, [Jesus] interpreted to them in all the Scriptures the things concerning himself. (Luke 24:27)

As we study Scripture, we want to be careful not to overspiritualize what we read by assigning symbolic meaning to every object, number, event, person, and so on in the Bible. As our understanding of Scripture grows, we'll find it easier to recognize actual types and symbols. Until then, it's helpful to confirm our interpretation by consulting a few commentaries to see how Christ's church has historically interpreted the passage.

PRACTICE SESSION: MARK 11:12–12:12

Mark 11:12–25

INTENT

- Mark creates a Markan Sandwich in verses 12–25. He sandwiches Jesus's visit to the temple on each side with a parable of a fig tree.
- Parables point to the kingdom of God and lay a simple illustration next to the spiritual truth it spotlights, which in today's passage is the scene in the temple.
- Fig trees in ancient Israel produced two crops of fruit. The early fruit (edible buds called *paggim*) appeared at the same time as the leaves.[14] A fig tree with leaves but no fruit was like someone who made promises they didn't keep.
- Each year, all Israel came to Jerusalem to celebrate Passover and find forgiveness through the Passover lamb. And throughout the year, God's people came to the temple to pray and offer sacrifices to obtain forgiveness.
- The court of the Gentiles was the only place the temple leaders allowed non-Jews to worship God and pray in the temple area. Money changers and merchants filled this court.
- The original pattern for the tabernacle, which was the temple's

prototype, had no division between Jews and Gentiles (see Numbers 15:14–16).
- The context of Mark 11:23 identifies "this mountain" as the Mount of Olives, which will be split by an earthquake when Christ returns (Zechariah 14:4).
- In Mark 11:23, Jesus is not promising we can make God do whatever we want as long as we pray with enough faith. He uses hyperbole to encourage greater faith in God, which overflows into bold prayer (James 1:6–8).
- Most manuscripts don't include verse 26.

TRUTH

Pray and read Mark 11:12–25. As you follow Christ in today's passage, remember why God gave His people the temple and why He sent Jesus. Notice how Jesus intricately connects the fig tree, the temple, and His command to pray bold prayers. Remember the Truth questions and make notes about the snapshots in today's passage.

TRIUNE GOD	OTHERS
	DISCIPLES
	FIG TREE
	TEMPLE

- What did Jesus come to the fig tree to find?

- What did Jesus pronounce over the fig tree?

- What did people come to the temple to obtain?

- What did Jesus's actions pronounce over the temple?

- If the temple is "withered," where will people go to pray and find forgiveness? (Hint: John 2:19–21.)

Mark 11:27–12:12

INTENT

- Jesus emphasizes the spiritual truths revealed in His visual parable of the fig tree and His corresponding verbal parable of the vineyard.

TRUTH

Pray and read Mark 11:27–12:12. Continue to follow Jesus back into the temple. Consider the full context. What does each main character in the parable of the vineyard symbolize? What spiritual truth does this parable emphasize? How does this spiritual truth reflect the kingdom of God? How does God call us to respond?

TRIUNE GOD	OTHERS
	VINEYARD OWNER
	VINEYARD TENANTS
	OWNER'S SERVANTS/SON

TRANSFORMATION

The snapshot of my husband, Larry, captured an accurate reflection of his kindness. He's a picture of God's amazing grace both in his life and in mine.

If someone could capture in a photograph what it looks like to trust Christ, how much would the snapshot resemble us? Too many times I've been a snapshot of what it looks like to proclaim Christ but be a fruitless tree, withered with fears and discontentment—or rebellion. Thanks be to God, there's grace for those who come to Christ—the true Temple—and pray for forgiveness. He makes all who trust in Him abound in fruit in every season. And in every season, God is making us more like the image of Christ.

TRANSFORMATIONAL TRUTH

Christ makes all who trust in Him abound in fruit in every season. And in every season, God is making us more like the image of Christ.

Add to or review your Attributes of God list at the back of the book.

If you truly believe the truths revealed in today's passage, what will it look like for your fruitfulness to increase? In what areas will your life become a more consistent snapshot of Christ's pure and spotless bride? Journal your response.

TRANSFORMATIONAL BIBLE STUDY PRINCIPLES

- ✓ Throughout the Bible, God created snapshots—types, patterns, illustrations, shadows, and the like—to teach important spiritual truths, particularly about Christ and His kingdom.
- ✓ Avoid overspiritualizing Scripture. Don't assign symbolic meaning to every object, number, event, person, and so on in the Bible.

MEMORY VERSE: PROVERBS 9:10

Write out this week's memory verse.

WEEK FIVE — day three

Epistles

TODAY'S READING

Mark 12:13–37

I can still feel the sorrow when I realized that during our last move I'd lost two of my greatest earthly treasures: two letters—one from Mom and the other from Dad, both written shortly before they died. On separate occasions, for different reasons, they'd written to encourage me in their love. Whenever the pain of missing them overwhelmed me, I'd pull out their letters and let their words wrap their arms around me.

And now they were gone. First my parents. Then their letters of love.

LETTERS OF PERFECT LOVE

God created the letter-writing tradition and left us with twenty-one epistles—twenty-one letters of love from Him written through the hands of faithful men. Those men wrote out of deep emotion, like fathers who want their words to touch their children's hearts, effect change, and remind them of their heavenly Father's love.

HOW TO UNDERSTAND THE EPISTLES

The ancient epistles are similar to letters today. Most open with a greeting followed by the body of the letter and a conclusion. If an epistle doesn't follow the customary letter format, search the letter's content to determine why. The difference is intentional.

To understand the epistle's intended message, consider the context—and guard against assumptions. Each letter was written *to* a specific church or individual but *for* believers (not unbelievers) in every generation. Determine the author's original audience and the questions, needs, or challenges the letter addressed, such as false teaching. Look for hints in the greeting and closing.

Find and follow the author's structure and logic to its intended conclusion. Many epistles address the audience's needs by first explaining, "This is what Christ has done," and then, "This is how we respond."

Mark is a gospel narrative, not an epistle, but as in many epistles, we'll see Jesus answer questions and refute false teaching.

PRACTICE SESSION: MARK 12:13–37

INTENT

- The Herodians were a religious group who supported Rome.
- The Pharisees despised Rome and all who supported Rome.
- The Sadducees denied there is a resurrection, either in Jesus's day or in the end times. They also denied the authority of any Scripture other than the five books of Moses (Genesis–Deuteronomy).
- "They" in verse 13 refers to "the chief priests and the scribes and the elders" in Mark 11:27.
- The verb "trap" in verse 13 was often used to describe wild animals tracking their prey.[15]
- The Greek word for "test" in verse 15 is the same word used for Satan's tempting Jesus in the wilderness.
- Mark 12:24–27 is a chiasm.

TRUTH

Pray and read Mark 12:13–37. Feel the tension rise as opposition to Jesus increases. Listen to His opponents seek to trap Jesus in His words. Through the parley of questions and answers, what does Jesus expose about His opponents and teach His disciples—and us?

TRIUNE GOD	OTHERS

- In Mark 12:13–14, the Pharisees and Herodians come together to trap Jesus by pretending to pose a sincere question. If Jesus answers yes, the crowds may see Jesus as a supporter of Rome and turn against Him. If Jesus answers no, He'll be guilty of treason and ripe for a Roman cross. How did Jesus's questions expose the true condition of their hearts and His divine wisdom? How does Jesus's answer give you hope in our world today?

_____
_____
_____
_____
_____

- In Mark 12:18–27, what purpose could the Sadducees have for posing a question to Jesus involving a case study about the resurrection, which they don't believe in?

- How does Jesus's response in vv. 24–27 expose their hearts and guide ours? How does His answer give you hope in our world today?

- Where will an authentic desire for understanding truth and the power of God always lead us? (See v. 24.)

- How well do you know the Scriptures and the power of God? Could Jesus ask you the question He asked the Sadducees in verse 26: "Have you not read?" What will you do to make studying the Bible a continued habit?

- In Mark 12:28–34, a single scribe questions Jesus. Why do you think Jesus says to him, "You are not *far* from the kingdom of God" versus "Welcome to the kingdom of God"?

_____

_____

The temple leaders loved their religious system more than God. Their eyes were so fixed on themselves that they had no true understanding of their sin. We cannot enter the kingdom of God if we feel we have even a glimmer of righteousness of our own. We'll never truly trust Christ for our salvation until we see ourselves for who we truly are—and Christ for who He truly is.

The scribe is close. He understands that fully loving God with our hearts is greater than anything we can do with our hands or feet. But he sees, in a sense, "trees walking" (Mark 8:24). He doesn't see the depth of his sin, and he doesn't truly see Jesus—yet.

- In Mark 12:35–37, Jesus reveals who He truly is. The crowds listen with delight. If they truly understood, how do you think they'd logically respond?

_____

_____

TRANSFORMATION

I treasured my parents' letters because they knew me well and loved me still. There's no feeling like being fully known and loved *anyway.*

My heartbreaking loss took a happy turn about five years after our move when I stumbled across an unopened box in my attic. My parents' letters! The joy I felt as I pressed them against my heart remains with me today.

God gave us His letters of perfect love through the epistle writers—and the gospel of Mark—so that

> according to the riches of his glory he may grant [us] to be strengthened with power through his Spirit in [our] inner being, so that Christ may dwell in [our] hearts

through faith—that [we], being rooted and grounded in love, may have strength to comprehend with all the saints what is the breadth and length and height and depth, and to know the love of Christ that surpasses knowledge, that [we] may be filled with all the fullness of God. (Ephesians 3:16–19)

All of this love God has for us isn't because we deserve it but because in Christ He loves us anyway. (One word—*anyway*. Not two—*any way*. There's only one way to God—through Jesus Christ.)

TRANSFORMATIONAL TRUTH

In Christ, God loves us anyway.

Add to or review your Attributes of God list at the back of the book.

If you truly believe in Christ's perfect love for you, what will it look like in your life? How will trusting in His love destroy hypocrisy in your life? What will it look like today and tomorrow to walk in the power of God with grateful obedience? Journal your response.

_____
_____
_____
_____
_____
_____
_____
_____

_____

_____

_____

_____

TRANSFORMATIONAL BIBLE STUDY PRINCIPLES
- ✓ The epistles are letters much like a letter from a loving father to encourage and instruct his children with what Christ has done and how we should respond.
- ✓ Find and follow the logic of the epistles to their intended conclusion.

MEMORY VERSE: PROVERBS 9:10

Write out this week's memory verse.

WEEK FIVE — *day four*

Interpretation and Response

TODAY'S READING

Mark 12:35–13:2

Have you ever read something you wrote, but then when you read it again you have no idea what you meant? You struggle to interpret your own writing? I've had this experience many times. God never has.

ONE CORRECT INTERPRETATION—MANY RESPONSES

I may not be able to interpret my own writing all the time, but God always knows what He meant by what He said. Our job is to discover what God means, not dictate His one true meaning—or what we think He *should* mean according to current cultural sensitivities.

Once we've discerned, to the best of our ability, what God means, we must respond. The possibilities of how we can rightly respond to the correct interpretation are as individual as we are.

Humility is indispensable when we interpret the Bible. The finest Christian minds don't all agree on the correct interpretation of every text. The things on which we must agree are the gospel and the primary doctrines of the Bible; those we must get right. There's only one way to salvation: as Jesus said, "Repent and believe in the gospel" (Mark 1:15; 1 Corinthians 15:1–10; Ephesians 2:8–9). But as we seek to understand what God intended us to know and believe about non-gospel passages, we can humbly work through differing opinions on the interpretation.

In today's lesson, we'll look at a passage that has a popular interpretation. But is it the correct one?

PRACTICE SESSION: MARK 12:35–13:2

INTENT

Through Moses, God commanded Israel never to mistreat widows, or the people would suffer His burning wrath (Exodus 22:22–24; Deuteronomy 24:17–22).

TRUTH

Pray and read Mark 12:35–13:2. Place yourself into the scene. Look through their eyes. Don't put words or opinions into Jesus's mouth. Listen to His exact words, starting with His warnings about the scribes.

TRIUNE GOD	OTHERS

- In verse 40, what did Jesus say would happen to the scribes who acted as if they cared for poor widows but then confiscated their homes for financial gain?

- In verses 41–44, Jesus points out the individuals who gave an offering.

    Does Jesus commend or criticize the amount of money given? Or does He simply state the size of their offerings?

    Does Jesus state the attitude or motivation of either the rich or the widow when they gave? Do we truly know why either gave?

    Did Jesus instruct the disciples to give like the widow?

    After Jesus says the temple leaders like to "devour widows' houses," he says the widow gave all she had to live on. In the full context of today's passage, is it logical that Jesus would rejoice over a poor widow giving her last penny and going home with nothing with which to buy food? Why or why not?

In the next two verses (Mark 13:1–2), Mark records the disciples marveling at the beauty of the temple, followed by Jesus's foretelling its destruction.
    Consider the full context:

- Jesus's warnings and rebukes in surrounding verses of the corrupt religious leaders.
- Mark's focus on Jesus's training His disciples to faithfully serve and shepherd His church.
- God's warnings in Exodus 22 and Deuteronomy 24. (See Intent section.)

Place a check mark beside whichever interpretation seems more logical.

___Mark 12:41–44 is about following the widow's example and giving everything we have in the offering.

___Mark 12:41–44 is about Jesus's warning and condemnation of the religious leaders who used their position for financial gain and ignored God's command to shepherd His sheep and care for poor widows, not fleece them.

If the correct interpretation of the text is Christ's judgment on those who use His name to break His commands and fleece the poor for financial gain, list five ways we can rightly respond to this message. I'll start.

1. If we're treated unfairly, we can trust that God sees and will care for us.

2. _____

3. _____

4. _____

5. _____

TRANSFORMATION

Sometimes I say one thing but mean the exact opposite. God perfectly communicated His Word to each author. He knows what He meant every time. We, on the other hand, have to examine God's Word with lots of humility and care to draw out the correct interpretation. Even as we do our best, we're going to get it wrong at times. You may feel I've got it wrong in this lesson. Maybe I did.

The point of this lesson is twofold:

1. Recognize that God's interpretation of the text is always the right interpretation. We do our best to discern His meaning by keeping the text in its context and following the logic. But in the end, we could still be wrong. Seek to be right. Always be humble.
2. Recognize that while there's only one right interpretation, the one God intends, there are numerous ways to respond to it.

I mentioned earlier that one right way to respond to today's passage is to trust that God will care for us even when others mistreat us. We can also join a faithful church that follows Christ's commands and cares for the poor. We can avoid churches whose leaders get rich off their members. We can freely and wisely give to our church without fear for our financial future. We can determine to never take advantage of anyone, always follow Christ's commands, and glorify Him in all we do.

TRANSFORMATIONAL TRUTH

Seek to be right. Always be humble.

Add to or review your Attributes of God list at the back of the book.

Depending on how you interpret today's passage, if you truly believe the spiritual truths, how will you respond? What will it look like in your life to respond with true belief? Journal your response.

TRANSFORMATIONAL BIBLE STUDY PRINCIPLES

- ✓ Every text of Scripture has one correct interpretation—God's—and almost endless ways to rightly respond to it.
- ✓ Humility is vital when interpreting the Bible.

MEMORY VERSE: PROVERBS 9:10

Write out this week's memory verse.

WEEK FIVE — *day five*

Visionary Genre

TODAY'S READING

Mark 13:3–37

Want to know what Satan fears?

> And though this world, with devils filled,
> Should threaten to undo us,
> We will not fear, for God hath willed
> His truth to triumph through us:
> The Prince of Darkness grim,
> We tremble not for him;
> His rage we can endure,
> For lo! his doom is sure,
> One little word shall fell him.
> —Martin Luther, "A Mighty Fortress Is Our God"

PROPHECY AND APOCALYPTIC LITERATURE

Prophecy both forthtells and foretells. Apocalyptic literature (from the Greek word that means "an uncovering") reveals hidden mysteries through figurative language.

When God's people needed a message of warning or encouragement, God's authors used prophecy to *forthtell* His message. When they needed to know what would happen in the fullness of time, His authors *foretold* the future through prophecy and apocalyptic literature.

Through the visionary genres, God proclaims and displays Satan's doom in living color and torrid detail. Even greater, God displays the greatness of His own majesty and declares the magnitude of His works with poetic beauty and power. He calls His people to their knees in holy fear and repentance and to greater heights of faith and hope in His mercy, love, and faithfulness.

UNDERSTANDING VISIONARY GENRES

Perhaps no other genres result in more differing interpretations than prophecy and apocalyptic literature. Diving into the details is beyond the scope of this study. These four points, however, will get you started.

1. Visionary genres often use storytelling techniques with setting, characters, and action—but no plot. No beginning, middle, or end. They're like movie trailers or clips of dreams in which our world mixes with the supernatural world.
2. Like all Scripture, the text needs to be understood in its full context.
3. The visionary genres are more concerned with the message than with chronological order.
4. Assume the author meant what he said unless the context makes it clear he's using symbolism or figurative language. When John sees an otherworldly creature with seven heads and ten horns in Revelation 13:1, we can be certain John is using figurative language.

Today's passage contains typical prophetic language, with apocalyptic elements that reveal mysteries and catastrophic events. But it lacks the more figurative language and fantastical creatures you'd expect from a typical apocalypse.

PRACTICE SESSION: MARK 13:3–37

INTENT

- Jesus sits (the typical position of a king and teacher) on the Mount of Olives (the scene of end-time events—Zechariah 14:4) and delivers what is known as the Olivet Discourse.
- In Mark 13:13, the phrase "the one who endures to the end" doesn't mean Christians can lose their salvation. The Holy Spirit seals us for eternity and empowers us to display the evidence of our salvation—perseverance despite suffering.

- In Mark 13:14, Jesus takes an apocalyptic turn, and Mark interjects a message to us, the reader. Jesus is now talking to all believers.

TRUTH

Read Mark 13:3–37. Sit with Jesus on the Mount of Olives as He talks about future events. Envision everything He says as if you were there. Notice what He says and doesn't say.

TRIUNE GOD	OTHERS

- How can Jesus, who is our all-knowing God, not know the exact date of the end times?

It's mind-breaking to grasp how Christ is both fully God and fully man, aka the God-man. Jesus is one person with the Father and Holy Spirit

(Mark 12:29), but as God incarnate, He's veiled in flesh. Alongside His divine nature, Jesus possessed a human nature, yet one without sin, since He was conceived by the Holy Spirit. Joseph wasn't Jesus's biological father.

As God, Jesus knows all things. As man, He temporarily gave up His rights to the use of His divine attributes, being directed instead by the Father (John 5:19). After Jesus ascended to heaven, He returned to His former glory—to the full use of His divine nature—while still retaining His human nature as a man (John 17:5).

- What phrase does Jesus repeat in Mark 13:9, 23, and 33?

- What phrase does He repeat in Mark 13:33, 34, 35, and 37?

- Regardless of whether or not we can understand exactly when the end times will begin, we clearly know what Jesus wants us to do while we wait. He told us seven times. What does He want us to do?

TRANSFORMATION

The day of Christ's return, when His judgment will fall on all evil, is drawing nearer every day. Be on guard. Stay awake. But let Satan tremble, not you. Christ has declared his doom.

No matter what you face, you have Christ and all His promises. Rest in His safety as you love and serve Him with all your heart, soul, mind, and strength.

Fix your eyes on Christ and do not fear. Satan's rage we can endure. One little word shall fell him. Τετέλεσται (*tetelestai*): "It is finished" (John 19:30).

TRANSFORMATIONAL TRUTH

Be on guard. Stay awake. But let Satan tremble, not you. You have Christ and all His promises.

Add to or review your Attributes of God list at the back of the book.

If you truly believe what God has revealed in today's passage, what will it look like in your life to stay awake and be on guard? To fix your eyes on Christ and serve and love Him and your neighbor? What habits will you form—or break? Journal your response.

TRANSFORMATIONAL BIBLE STUDY PRINCIPLES

- ✓ Prophecy *forthtells* and *foretells*.
- ✓ Apocalyptic literature reveals hidden mysteries through figurative language.
- ✓ Visionary genres often use storytelling techniques with setting, characters, and action—but no plot—and are more concerned with the message than with chronology.
- ✓ Keep the text in its full context.
- ✓ Assume the author meant what he said, unless the context makes it clear he's using symbolism or figurative language.

MEMORY VERSE: PROVERBS 9:10

Write out this week's memory verse.

WEEK SIX

Follow Your *King*

MARK 14:1–16:8

Sanctify them in the truth; your word is truth.
—John 17:17

WEEK SIX — *day one*

Christ's Love and His Church

TODAY'S READING
Mark 14:1–11

Describe your church in one sentence.

PURE LOVE

Christ calls the church His bride and His family (Revelation 21:9; Mark 3:35). He trained His disciples for three years to prepare them to establish and build His church. Christ's love for His bride, the church, is the purest of loves—and it's the love He's called us to share with our brothers and sisters in Christ.

When you described your church, did you mention love or family?

The church is God's design for all believers. She's essential. Christ died for her. As a church, we're to come together to devote ourselves to the Bible's teaching, to fellowship, to the Lord's Supper, and to prayer (Acts 2:42). Unless we're physically unable to attend church (such as sick or out of town), we're not to stay home and hold sofa church in pj's with a livestream feed.

This modern trend of hunkering at home and "doing church" online opposes God's design and hurts us and our church. Isolation encourages us to focus on ourselves and withholds our service and fellowship from our church family, who are also called to love and serve us.

We need each other.

God calls us to "consider how to stir up one another to love and good works, *not neglecting to meet together, as is the habit of some*, but encouraging one another, and all the more as you see the Day drawing near" (Hebrews 10:24–25, emphasis mine).

What does the church have to do with effective Bible study? Everything. Christ gave us the church to equip us, build us up in love, and mature us in knowing and reflecting Him and serving Him and His people (Ephesians 4:11–16).

Part of the church's work is to help its members understand Scripture. When we combine personal Bible study with weekly expository (verse-by-verse) preaching and mutual encouragement through fellowship, our understanding of God and His Word can flourish and our love for Christ grow. Together, we'll more accurately reflect the heart of Christ, and we'll love Him with the level of gratefulness we witness in the woman in today's passage.

PRACTICE SESSION: MARK 14:1–11

INTENT

- Today's passage is a chiasm. Some scholars consider it a Markan Sandwich. The center spotlights the main message.
  A^1—The temple leaders secretly plot to murder Jesus.
      B—The woman anoints Jesus with expensive fragrant oil.
  A^2—Judas secretly offers to betray Jesus.
- The flask of fragrant oil was worth more than a full year's wage.

TRUTH

Pray and read Mark 14:1–11. Feel the stark contrast between the deep hatred that moved "men of God" to plot Jesus's murder and the soaring adoration of the woman in this passage. Smell the fragrant oil waft from her flask as the men's snarling rebukes clash with Jesus's compassion. Imagine the woman's relief, and the men's surprise, when He rebukes the men and defends and encourages her. Note the truths today's passage reveals about both the men and the woman, but more importantly, about our triune God.

TRIUNE GOD	OTHERS

- Each chiastic section contains a revealing, gut-punch statement. What do these statements reveal about the men's hearts and what they worshiped?

Mark 14:1

Mark 14:4

Mark 14:11

- The woman poured out all the oil—all its worth. She gave it all to Jesus. How easy would it be for you to pour out $50,000, even onto Jesus? Write more about your answer.

- Are you willing to pour out all your pride and humble yourself for Christ? When you feel wronged, are you willing to die to your right to be offended and turn the other cheek? Are you willing to trust Christ like this woman—and forgive others like Christ forgave you? If not, what's holding you back?

_____

_____

_____

Jesus's disciples—the men who confessed Him as Messiah—rebuked the woman for "wasting" the costly oil on Jesus. We're not surprised Judas saw such worship of Jesus as a waste. Judas was a thief (John 12:6). He didn't love Jesus or care for the poor. He lusted after more money to pilfer from the money bag. But the other disciples? How could they see *anything* as being "wasted" on Jesus? I wonder how often our words or actions echo this unspeakable thought.

The greatest commandment is to love the Lord with all our heart, soul, mind, and strength (Mark 12:29–30). Let us eagerly "waste" our time, talents, and possessions—our pure nard—on Jesus as a natural outpouring of our love for Him.

- Do you have someone in your church whose life teaches you what it looks like to be purely devoted to Christ like the woman in today's passage? If not, be that person in your church. If you do, surprise them with a letter to encourage and thank them for their example—and then follow their example.

TRANSFORMATION

Some disciples stood with their mouths agape at the "waste" of such valuable treasure dripping off Jesus's head. What do you value more than Jesus? Your time? Resources? Sunday morning sleep? Or do you delight to "waste" yourself in reading and studying His Word, serving His church, and ministering with the gospel in the world?

Seek to know the Lord and pour out all your worship. He is worthy. And love His church, which He died to save.

TRANSFORMATIONAL TRUTH

A life "wasted" for Christ is a fragrant aroma to the Lord.

Add to or review your Attributes of God list at the back of the book.

How do the truths of today's passage convict and/or encourage your heart? What will it look like in your life to love Christ with the same level of devotion as the woman? How will your worship overflow into love for your church? Journal your response.

_____
_____
_____
_____
_____
_____
_____
_____
_____
_____
_____

TRANSFORMATIONAL BIBLE STUDY PRINCIPLES

- ✓ The church is essential in the Christian life. She's God's design for all believers. Wholeheartedly join and serve your fellow members.
- ✓ Through church, we come together to devote ourselves to the Bible's teaching, to fellowship, to the Lord's Supper, and to prayer (Acts 2:42).
- ✓ Delight to "waste" yourself in reading and studying God's Word, serving His church, and ministering with the gospel in the world.

MEMORY VERSE

Write out this week's memory verse and read it out loud five times.

Sanctify them in the truth; your word is truth. (John 17:17)

Fruitfulness

TODAY'S READING

Mark 14:12–42

Jesus looked at His disciples. "One of you will betray me."

Imagine the flood of emotions that crashed against the disciples. Surely they thought, "We've left everything to follow you, Jesus. Why would any of us betray you?"

Whatever concerns Judas may have had, they weren't enough to halt his plan. But his evil scheme served only to advance God's redemptive purpose. God's Word will be accomplished.

> So shall my word be that goes out from my mouth;
>   it shall not return to me empty,
> but it shall accomplish that which I purpose,
>   and shall succeed in the thing for which I sent it.
>   (Isaiah 55:11)

GOD'S WORD WILL ACCOMPLISH HIS PURPOSES

Just as the prophets foretold in the Old Testament, Judas would betray Christ (Psalm 41:9), and Christ would redeem us on the cross (Isaiah 53:4–5). All God's Word will be fulfilled just as it was written. This promise also means that if you belong to Christ, you *will* be fruitful, and you will become more like Christ (John 15:5; Romans 8:29).

As with Jesus's disciples, our understanding of truth will be wonky at times—or flat-out wrong—but God will correct our misunderstanding as we continue to seek to know the truth and depend on the Holy Spirit to teach us.

Let the faithfulness of God's Word fuel your drive to be a faithful student of the Bible and disciple of Christ. Pick up your Bible and study it, and pick up your cross and follow Christ (Matthew 16:24). Neither Christ nor His Word can fail. Mark spotlights this truth in today's passage as we watch those who should love Christ betray Him instead—just as it was written (Zechariah 11:12).

PRACTICE SESSION: MARK 14:12–42

INTENT

- Today's passage is a chiasm. In every grouping, either we see Jesus prophesy or we see a prophecy fulfilled.
  - A^1 Judas goes to the temple leaders to betray Jesus. (14:10–11)
    - B^1 Jesus sends His disciples to prepare Passover. (vv. 12–16)
      - C^1 Jesus prophesies one of His disciples will betray Him. (vv. 17–21)
        - **D Jesus gives His disciples bread and wine as His body and blood. (vv. 22–25)**
      - C^2 Jesus prophesies His disciples will fall away, and Peter will deny Him. (vv. 26–31)
    - B^2 Jesus takes His disciples into the garden to pray. (vv. 32–39)
  - A^2 Jesus rises to meet Judas, His betrayer. (vv. 40–42)
- Jesus uses metaphors to symbolize the bread as His body and the cup (the fruit of the vine) as His blood. Both are symbols of the new covenant of grace for those who will believe.

TRUTH

Pray and read Mark 14:12–42. Wonder with the disciples as they go into the city to prepare for Passover and find everything just as Jesus says. Experience the disciples' distress that one of them will betray Jesus and their confusion as He gives them the bread and cup. Feel Jesus's deep agony in the garden as He prays and His determination as He rises to go meet His betrayer.

TRIUNE GOD	OTHERS

What is the central theme of today's passage? (Look at the center of the chiasm.) How does everything build up to and off of this verse?

_____

_____

_____

_____

Jesus poured out such agony in His prayer that His sweat was like drops of blood falling to the ground (Luke 22:44). In His humanity, Jesus felt the full horror of the cup He must drink. Three times He prayed from the depths of His anguish, but each time, He aligned His heart with the will of His Father.

- How do Jesus's prayers help you understand how to pray through your deepest trials?

___

___

___

When the time appointed in eternity past arrived, Jesus wiped away the sweat, went to His sleeping disciples, and said, "Rise, let us go. See, My betrayer is approaching!" (Mark 14:42 BSB).

- How does Jesus's willingness to pick up His cross and fall into the hands of His enemies to suffer the vilest evil in history challenge or encourage you in your trial today?

___

___

___

Because Jesus's will was to do God's will, He rose from His night of fervent prayer to meet His betrayer and accept the cup He must drink for our salvation—just as it was written. Jesus fixed His eyes forward to another cup—a glorious cup filled with joy that He will drink with His bride, the church, at the marriage supper of the Lamb (Mark 14:25).

> The angel said to me, "Write this: Blessed are those who are invited to the marriage supper of the Lamb." And he said to me, "These are the true words of God." (Revelation 19:9)

TRANSFORMATION

What God has written will be accomplished. None of His promises will fail.

If you belong to Christ, you *will* grow in the love and understanding of God's Word (Psalm 119:103; 1 Peter 2:2–3).

Why not choose now to study God's Word and know what is written rather than wait for God to bring you to your knees in surrender?

You *will* follow Christ's footsteps and become like Him (Romans 8:29).

Why not choose now to fix your eyes on Him, pick up your cross, and follow Him rather than pitch your cross and flee?

God *will* give you the desire and the power to do what pleases Him (Philippians 2:13). It's only a matter of time. Why not now?

Rise, let us go.

TRANSFORMATIONAL TRUTH

Study and pray, then rise and obey.

Add to or review your Attributes of God list at the back of the book.

If you truly believe what Christ has promised and revealed about His Word and His will through today's passage, what will it look like in your life? How will it change the way you study and pray, and rise and obey? How will it move you to pick up your cross and follow Christ? Journal your response.

_____

_____

_____

_____

_____

_____

_____

_____

_____

_____

_____

TRANSFORMATIONAL BIBLE STUDY PRINCIPLES

✓ You won't always interpret God's Word correctly. Continue to seek the truth and trust the Holy Spirit to teach and correct you.
✓ All God's Word will be fulfilled just as it was written.

MEMORY VERSE: JOHN 17:17

Write out this week's memory verse.

WEEK SIX — day three

Belief

TODAY'S READING

Mark 14:43–72

It's funny how confident we can be in how we'd respond to certain situations, only to respond opposite of what we'd imagined. A friend was confident her husband would laugh when she jumped out of her hiding place and yelled, "Boo!" He fainted instead. That's funny (since he didn't get hurt). But when I think how often I've been confident about the depth of my faith but then responded as if Jesus and His promises didn't even exist, I realize it's not always funny. Sometimes it's deeply alarming.

CHECK FAITH ALERTS

Part of effective Bible study is checking to see how we're responding in life to the truth we're learning as we study. Whenever we respond to circumstances with anxiety, anger, or any of their emotional cousins rather than confident faith, God uses our troubling reaction as a flashing "check faith" alert. We need to check the level of one or more of three faith issues.

1. **Knowledge.** There's something about God we don't yet fully (or correctly) understand that would settle our emotions in Him.
   Pray and ask God to reveal what you still need to learn about His character, nature, or the ways He works.
2. **Belief.** We know the truth that defeats our troubled emotions, but we struggle to truly believe—at least in this moment. *If*

onlys, What ifs, or *Oh, no, you didn'ts* tempt us to forget or doubt the truth we know.

Pray and ask God to reveal the lie you're believing and to remind you of the truth that destroys the lies. Trust God and His Word, not your emotions or doubts.

3. **Rebellion.** We know the truth, but we don't like it because we want what we want. Our pride convinces us we know better than God what's good and right and what will make us truly happy.

Ask God to show you the root of your pride and the lie that's feeding your emotions and controlling your response. Remind yourself who God is, repent of your rebellion, and walk in the truth—no matter the cost.

PRACTICE SESSION: MARK 14:53–72

INTENT

- Today's passage includes a chiasm and a Markan Sandwich. The center of the chiasm is Jesus's confident proclamation of who He is (Mark 14:62). The Markan Sandwich interrupts the scene of Peter by the fire with the scene of Jesus before the Sanhedrin.
- Many believe Mark could be the unnamed man who fled without his linen cloth.
- The title "Christ" comes from the Greek word for "Messiah," the anointed Savior (and "Son of the Blessed").

TRUTH

Pray and read Mark 14:53–72. Since this lesson focuses on checking for faith alerts, I didn't include a Truth chart, but I encourage you to study the passage with the Truth questions in mind.

As you read, reach for the warmth of the fire as the chill of Peter's fears and the icy hatred of Jesus's enemies surround you. Feel the Sanhedrin's frustration as their false witnesses fail to agree. Hear Jesus speak His only words and watch the ensuing chaos. In the distance, hear a rooster crow twice, and feel Peter's hot tears burn your soul.

Study each person's actions and check his faith level according to the three faith issues above. I'll start.

Peter

My observations: Peter's confidence that he'll never abandon Jesus is rock solid, the kind of foundation you can build a church on—until Judas shows up with a crowd armed with clubs and swords. Peter grabs a sword and slices off the ear of the high priest's servant (as if Jesus can't handle the situation). What we truly believe about Jesus determines the weapons we'll choose for warfare. Worldly weapons destroy; Scripture, the "sword of the Spirit," saves.

Peter careens through the events of the night like a boulder crashing down a mountain. Peter has seen and heard all he needs to know about Jesus; nevertheless, he falls into momentary unbelief, most likely driven by fear of being arrested. The solution is to remember and believe what Christ has said—which Peter does the moment a rooster crows twice.

Jesus takes Peter where he doesn't want to go (Mark 14:27–31) to get him where he needs to be—grounded in the truth (Mark 14:72).

Those are my thoughts about Peter. Now it's your turn for the rest.

Judas. How does Judas reveal his arrogance, thinking he can seize and lead Jesus where He doesn't already intend to go? What does this reveal about Judas's faith issues?

Jewish Sanhedrin. Consider how Jesus fulfills Isaiah 53:7, a prophecy the members of the Sanhedrin had surely memorized. Since they knew the Old Testament and its prophecies concerning Christ, what do their actions reveal about their faith issues?

_____

_____

_____

_____

_____

Roman Gentile Guards. The guards ironically fulfill Isaiah 50:6 when they demand Jesus prophesy who hit Him. What would you say this passage suggests about their faith issues?

_____

_____

_____

_____

_____

Jesus. In what ways does Jesus portray perfect faith?

_____

_____

_____

_____

TRANSFORMATION

Jesus's own people, represented in the Jewish leaders, didn't receive Him. Instead, they seized Him.

His disciples received Him, but they all failed and fled.

Christ remained confident in the Father.

The harder our circumstances, the more they expose the truth about what we truly believe about Jesus. We'll fail and flee or remain and stand on the truth depending on the level of our faith in the moment. No true believer wants to fail Christ or act like we don't know Him, but sometimes our failures are the only way we'll see the true condition of our faith. God uses our trials and failures to refine our faith.

TRANSFORMATIONAL TRUTH

Our trials expose and refine what we truly believe about Jesus.

Add to or review your Attributes of God list at the back of the book.

If you truly believe the blessings that come from having the true condition of our faith exposed, how will you respond in your trials?

What will it look like in your life to respond like Christ rather than like Peter? Journal your response.

_____

_____

_____

_____

_____

_____

_____

_____

TRANSFORMATIONAL BIBLE STUDY PRINCIPLES

- ✓ Part of effective Bible study is checking to see how we're responding in life to the truth we're learning as we study.
- ✓ We need to check our level of three faith issues: knowledge, belief, and rebellion.
    1. **Knowledge.** There's something about God we don't yet fully (or correctly) understand that would settle our emotions in Him.
    2. **Belief.** We know the truth that defeats our troubled emotions, but we struggle to truly believe—at least in this moment.
    3. **Rebellion.** We know the truth, but we don't like it because we want what we want.

MEMORY VERSE: JOHN 17:17

Write out this week's memory verse.

WEEK SIX — *day four*

Wholeness

TODAY'S READING

Mark 15:1–39

Guess how many verses in the Bible help explain today's passage.

At least five hundred.[16] (You read that right: 500.)

Does this vast number help you grasp the value of reading the whole Bible?

WHOLE BIBLE FAITH

Today I'm not introducing a new Bible study principle but proclaiming a needed reminder: read the Bible widely and study it deeply.

Reading gives us a breadth of knowledge that makes our studying more transformational.

Studying gives us a depth of knowledge that makes our reading more transformational. It's a beautiful symbiotic relationship.

As we read, we see the full picture of the Bible. We see the forest.

As we study, we see the individual trees and make deeper connections from one end of the Bible to the other.

Reading *and* studying both informs and transforms. God uses the whole Bible to build in us a whole faith. Understand, though, that our efforts are not what transform us. God's Word does. Invest in your faith by investing time in God's Word.

While studying a book of the Bible, don't skip your daily Bible reading.

While reading through the Bible, resist stopping to study everything you read. Make a note and study it later.

As you dive into studying a particular book, first immerse yourself only in that book. The author assumes you'll consider all Scripture as you study, but he's got a particular message to convey. Mark left out much the other gospels included. He gave only the details needed to convey the message God's Spirit directed him to deliver.

After we zero in on the author's main message, we're ready to soak in the author's message in its fuller, glorious context—the whole Bible. All parts of the Bible work together. We'll see this truth in today's passage.

PRACTICE SESSION: MARK 15:1–39

INTENT

- The name Barabbas means "son of the father." Barabbas, the guilty son of the father, was set free—but not by his power or persuasiveness. Jesus, *the* Son of the Father, took Barabbas's place on the cross, as He did for us.
- When God tore the curtain from top to bottom at Jesus's death, He removed the holy barrier between His people and Himself because Jesus was the final and perfect sacrifice. He declared the end of the sacrificial system.

TRUTH

Pray and read Mark 15:1–39. As you step into today's passage, let the crushing weight and searing pain of Christ's sacrifice for sinners wash over you. Note how the smug words and mocking actions of Jesus's enemies play right into God's plans and prophecies. Consider today's passage in light of what you know from the whole Bible.

TRIUNE GOD	OTHERS

- Write down the verse numbers from today's passage that the following verses prophesy about or otherwise spotlight. (Be glad we're not examining all five hundred verses that help explain today's passage!)

    _____ Exodus 10:21–23 (Darkness is often linked to judgment in the Bible.)

    _____ Numbers 21:7–9

    _____ Deuteronomy 21:22–23 (The cross was often called a tree in the Jewish culture; e.g., Acts 5:30; 10:39.)

_____ Psalm 22:1

_____ Isaiah 53:3

_____ Isaiah 53:4–6

_____ Isaiah 53:7

_____ Acts 3:14

_____ Romans 4:25

_____ Hebrews 10:19–20

_____ 1 Peter 2:23

_____ 1 Peter 3:18

TRANSFORMATION

Of Jesus's seven statements on the cross, Mark recorded only one—the statement that best portrays Jesus as the Suffering Servant and Son of God. Quoting the mournful words of King David, Jesus cried out, "My God, my God, why have you forsaken me?" (Psalm 22:1).

Jesus wasn't truly asking why God had forsaken Him as the sins of the world fell on Him. He knew why. Jesus, the Son of David (Matthew 1:1), was identifying with King David's anguish in one of the psalms that foreshadowed Christ and the cross.

The Jewish leaders, who had memorized Psalm 22, watched it play out before their eyes. But rather than recognizing this and feeling deep conviction, they felt only scorn for Jesus.

The Roman centurion had likely never read nor even heard of Psalm 22:1 or any of the Old Testament prophecies Jesus fulfilled on the cross. Yet, watching how Jesus breathed His last, the centurion's own breath caught in his throat. Never had he seen anyone die on the cross like this. Never had he heard anyone speak with such strength and then give up his spirit. He hadn't a clue he was witnessing the fulfillment of the prophecy in the garden of Eden. But what he saw when Jesus breathed His last shook him.

"Truly this man was the Son of God!" (Mark 15:39).

From first to last, from Genesis to Revelation, it's all about Christ. Read the Bible widely, study it deeply, and be transformed.

TRANSFORMATIONAL TRUTH

God uses the whole Bible to build in us a whole faith.

Add to or review your Attributes of God list at the back of the book.

If you truly believe the many truths today's passage reveals, how will you respond? What truths will fill your mind when evil seems to be winning? What will it look like in your life if you believe God uses the whole Bible to build in you a whole faith? How will your thoughts about the Old Testament change? How will your habits change? Journal your response.

TRANSFORMATIONAL BIBLE STUDY PRINCIPLES

- ✓ Read the Bible widely and study it deeply.
- ✓ Studying adds depth, which makes our reading more transformational. Reading adds breadth, which makes our studying more transformational.
- ✓ Our efforts don't transform us. God's Word does. Invest in your faith by investing time in God's Word.

MEMORY VERSE: JOHN 17:17

Write out this week's memory verse.

WEEK SIX — *day five*

Read, Study, and Live It Out

TODAY'S READING

Mark 15:40–16:8

In the still morning hours of the third day, Mary Magdalene, Mary the mother of James, and Salome meet with sorrowful hearts and spice-laden hands to walk to the tomb and anoint their Teacher's body. As they draw near, what they see halts their steps.

Who rolled the stone away?

The three women inch toward the tomb and step through the opening.

A man in a white robe startles them. "Don't be alarmed," he says.

How can they be anything but alarmed?

"You seek Jesus of Nazareth, who was crucified. He has risen; He is not here. See the place where they laid Him."

Risen?

How?

Where?

What does he mean?

The women lock eyes.

Can it be?

GO!

We've reached the end of our study and the gospel of Mark and ironically, the One we've been searching to know this whole study is not in the final scene. He's not here. He's risen—just as He said.

Jesus didn't come to stay. He came to go (John 14:1–3).

He came to go to the cross and give His life (Mark 10:33–34).

He came to go to Galilee and prove His resurrection and train His befuddled disciples (Mark 16:7).

And He came to go to His Father in heaven until the time is fulfilled and He comes again with the clouds of heaven (Mark 14:62).

My prayer for you now is that you will not stay where you are but that you too will go.

Go and walk in true belief of what God has said in His Word about who He is.

Believe in the power of the Father who has proclaimed His greatness and purposes.

Walk in the humility of Jesus, who demonstrated His love and salvation on the cross.

Depend on the Holy Spirit. He will empower you and help you study all God's Word, and He will keep and hold you forever.

Stoke your fervency to know the Lord on every page.

And respond. Live out what God has worked in you through His Word.

Go in the truth of God's Word, and never give up.

PRACTICE SESSION: MARK 15:40–16:8

INTENT

- Jewish law forbade a hung body to be left hanging overnight (Deuteronomy 21:22–23). Obedience to this law was all the more urgent for the Sabbath.
- Romans buried criminals with criminals except by special request.
- A woman's testimony wasn't admissible in court in ancient Israel.
- The other gospels record that the women obeyed the angel.
- Mark chose the following words to describe the women's reaction to Jesus's resurrection:

    Trembling (Greek *tromos*) describes "the anxiety of one who distrusts his ability completely to meet all requirements, but religiously does his utmost to fulfil his duty."[17]

Astonishment (Greek *ekstasis*) means "blended fear and wonderment."[18]

Afraid (Greek *phobeō*) can mean "to fear or be afraid" and "to reverence, venerate, to treat with deference or reverential obedience."[19]

- None of the earliest manuscripts include Mark 16:9–20. Most New Testament scholars believe a copyist added these verses later—perhaps because the ending felt too abrupt.

TRUTH

Pray and read Mark 15:40–16:8. Step into today's scene at the cross. Stand in the distance with the women and mourn Jesus's death. Follow Joseph of Arimathea as he lays Jesus's body, wrapped in fine linen, in his tomb. Hear the grating of the stone as it rolls in front of Jesus's tomb. On the third day, walk with the women in the early morning hours. Feel your heart race with confusion and wonder at what you find—and don't find—at the tomb.

TRIUNE GOD	OTHERS

- Compare Mark 1:1–3 with Mark 16:7–8. Each author chose how they would open and close their book. We compared these two verses in the first week of our study. Has your answer changed over the course of the study? What would you say Mark wants us to understand about Jesus and following Him? What kind of response to Jesus is Mark seeking?

_____
_____
_____
_____
_____
_____

- Read Isaiah 53:9. How did God fulfill this prophecy?

_____
_____

- Joseph of Arimathea was a prominent Sanhedrin council member and secret follower of Jesus (John 19:38). How do his actions show courage?

_____
_____

TRANSFORMATION

By the time Mark wrote this gospel, persecution in Rome had intensified. Peter had likely already been crucified upside down for his faith. Mark wrote to strengthen Christ's battered church. Like Joseph of Arimathea, who ignored the consequences he might suffer for honoring Jesus's dead body, Mark disregarded the risk to his life to record and spread the gospel of Jesus Christ.

Mark recorded the whole truth even though it meant including the inadmissible and "unacceptable" testimony of women to Jesus's resurrection.

Search your heart. What might you have done in each situation?

Leave Jesus's body to be tossed in a grave with criminals?

Play it safe, and walk away from following Christ?

Water down the truth to make God's Word more acceptable to more people?

Every day we make choices. The choices you make today affect your faith tomorrow. Choose to read and study the Bible. But don't just read it. Go, and live it out.

No matter how hard or how much you may tremble over what you face, choose to follow Christ. Choose to go and tell others what He has done for you—and them. Most won't believe you. Many will mock you and hate you because of Christ's name. Fear fades and confidence and peace rise the more the love of Christ rises in our hearts. He is with you—and He loves you.

Do not fear. Only believe.

And go!

TRANSFORMATIONAL TRUTH

The choices we make today affect our faith tomorrow.

Add to or review your Attributes of God list at the back of the book.

If you truly believe the truths God revealed in today's passage, what will it look like in your life? How will your heart be changed and your life be different tomorrow from having studied the gospel of Mark these past six weeks? Journal your response.

_____

_____

_____

_____

_____

_____

_____

_____

_____

_____

_____

TRANSFORMATIONAL BIBLE STUDY PRINCIPLES

- ✓ Stoke your fervency to know the Lord on every page of the Bible. And respond.
- ✓ Live out what God has worked in you through His Word.
- ✓ Go in the truth of God's Word, and never give up.

MEMORY VERSE

Review all six memory verses: 2 Peter 1:3; 2 Timothy 2:15; Psalm 119:18; Mark 9:7; Proverbs 9:10; John 17:17.

Attributes of God

Notes

1. Strong's, s.v., "G2316—theos," Blue Letter Bible, accessed July 1, 2024, https://www.blueletterbible.org/lexicon/g2316/kjv/tr/0-1/.
2. Strong's, s.v., "G2424—iēsous," Blue Letter Bible, accessed July 1, 2024, https://www.blueletterbible.org/lexicon/g2424/kjv/tr/0-1/.
3. Strong's, s.v., "G5547—christos," Blue Letter Bible, accessed July 1, 2024, https://www.blueletterbible.org/lexicon/g5547/kjv/tr/0-1/.
4. Strong's, s.v., "G3173—megas," Biblehub, accessed August 22, 2024, https://biblehub.com/greek/3173.htm.
5. Strong's, s.v., "G1169—deilos," Biblehub, accesssed August 22, 2024, https://biblehub.com/greek/1169.htm.
6. Strong's, "G5399—phobeó," Biblehub. accesssed August 22, 2024, https://biblehub.com/greek/5399.htm.
7. Sefaria.org, accessed August 21, 2024, https://www.sefaria.org/Mishnah_Ketubot.4.4?lang=bi&with=all&lang2=en.
8. Jonathan Peterson, "When Was Each Book of the Bible Written?," BibleGateway, February 1, 2016, https://www.biblegateway.com/blog/2016/02/when-was-each-book-of-the-bible-written/.
9. See Strong's, s.v., "G5526—chortazō," Blue Letter Bible, accessed September 8, 2024, https://www.blueletterbible.org/lexicon/g5526/esv/mgnt/0-1/.
10. This information is inspired by Leland Ryken's book *Sweeter Than Honey, Richer Than Gold: A Guided Study of Biblical Poetry* (Bellingham, WA: Lexham Press, 2015), 31.
11. Biblehub, https://biblehub.com/galatians/3-24.htm#lexicon.
12. Douglas Sean O'Donnell, *Mark*, vol. 3 of *Expository Reflections on the Gospels* (Wheaton: Crossway, 2024), 276–79.
13. The exact number varies depending on the translation, but the point

remains the same: Jesus asked people a lot of probing and revealing questions.

14. O'Donnell, *Mark*, 331.
15. Mark L. Strauss, *Mark*, vol. 2 of *Zondervan Exegetical Commentary on the New Testament* (Grand Rapids: Zondervan, 2014), 523.
16. I looked in *The New Treasury of Scripture Knowledge* (rev. ed, Jerome Smith, ed. [Nashville: Nelson, 2023]) and estimated the number of verses related to today's passage. This valuable resource lists verses and passages that relate to parallel or contrasting "thoughts, themes, doctrines, subjects, concepts, figures of speech, or literary motifs" of the words in each verse of Scripture.
17. Strong's, s.v., "G5156—tromos," Blue Letter Bible, accessed July 19, 2024, https://www.blueletterbible.org/lexicon/g5156/esv/mgnt/0-1/.
18. Strong's, s.v., "G1611—ekstasis," Blue Letter Bible, accessed July 19, 2024, https://www.blueletterbible.org/lexicon/g1611/esv/mgnt/0-1/.
19. Strong's, s.v., "G5399—phobeō," Blue Letter Bible, accessed July 19, 2024, https://www.blueletterbible.org/lexicon/g5399/esv/mgnt/0-1/.

Resources

I owe much gratitude to the authors of each of the following resources for their invaluable help in writing this study.

Ferguson, Sinclair B. *From the Mouth of God: Trusting, Reading, and Applying the Bible*. Edinburgh: Banner of Truth Trust, 2019.

———. *Let's Study Mark*. Edinburgh: The Banner of Truth Trust, 2020.

Goldsworthy, Graeme. *According to Plan: The Unfolding Revelation of God in the Bible*. Downers Grove, IL: IVP, 1991.

Hughes, R. Kent. *Mark, Volume One*. Westchester: Crossway, 1989.

———. *Mark, Volume Two*. Westchester: Crossway, 1989.

Keener, Craig S., and John H Walton, eds. *NKJV Cultural Backgrounds Study Bible*. Grand Rapids: Zondervan, 2017.

Lane, William L. *The Gospel According to Mark*. Grand Rapids: Eerdmans, 1974.

Minto, Dr. Marty. *Study the Word* podcast.

O'Donnell, Douglas Sean. *Expository Reflections on the Gospels: Mark*. Wheaton: Crossway, 2024.

O'Donnell, Douglas Sean, and Leland Ryken. *The Beauty and Power of Biblical Exposition: Preaching the Literary Artistry and Genres of the Bible*. Wheaton: Crossway, 2022.

Plummer, Robert L. *40 Questions About Interpreting the Bible*. Grand Rapids: Kregel, 2021.

Ryken, Leland. *A Complete Handbook of Literary Forms in the Bible*. Wheaton: Crossway, 2014.

———. *How to Read the Bible as Literature*. Grand Rapids: Zondervan Academic, 1984.

———. *Literary Introductions to the Books of the Bible*. Wheaton: Crossway, 2015.

———. *Sweeter Than Honey, Richer Than Gold: A Guided Study of Biblical Poetry*. Bellingham, WA: Lexham Press, 2015.

Ryken, Leland, and Philip Graham Ryken. *The Literary Study Bible*. Wheaton: Crossway, 2007.

Smith, Jerome H., ed. *The New Treasury of Scripture Knowledge*. Nashville: Nelson, 2023.

Sproul, R. C. *Everyone's a Theologian: An Introduction to Systematic Theology*. Sanford, FL: Ligonier Ministries, 2014.

———. *Knowing Scripture: Expanded Edition*. Downers Grove, IL: IVP, 2016.

Strauss, Mark L. *Mark*. Vol. 2 of *Exegetical Commentary on the New Testament*. Grand Rapids: Zondervan, 2014.

Zuck, Roy B. *Basic Bible Interpretation*. Colorado Springs: David C. Cook, 1991.

Thank You!

Thank you for taking this journey with me into what I pray will become (if it isn't already) one of your greatest joys in life—studying God's Word. I'm grateful to you for entrusting me with your time and with such an important and glorious topic as discovering God's Word.

I've been praying for you, that each word in this study will help ignite a passion in your heart to know Christ and His Word more each day. If you'd like to continue on this journey of Bible study with me, join me on my website, JeanWilund.com, and podcast, *It's All About Him!*

In addition to being grateful for you, my readers, my heart is overwhelmed with gratefulness to other special people who have walked this journey with me.

Above all, I thank my Lord and Savior Jesus Christ, who gave me life and a passion for His Word. All glory goes to Him and to the Father and Holy Spirit for any blessing and benefit anyone receives from this study.

To Dawn Anderson, Sarah De Mey, Melissa Wade, Kat Needham, and all those at Our Daily Bread Publishing, thank you for inviting me to write this study and for showing great patience with me as I wrestled with how to best structure it. Your encouragement, grace, and support mean more to me than you can know. I love being a part of this great ministry.

To Dr. Marty Minto, thank you for never holding back as you critiqued this study and helped ensure its theological faithfulness to Scripture. You and Renee remain two of my greatest encouragers. I couldn't have written this without you. Truly.

To Lori Hatcher, thank you for reading every lesson one more time and rushing to my side with your daily prayers and a family-sized bag of Reese's cups when the complexity of this study overwhelmed my ability to write it.

To my loyal critique group, Lisa, Lori, Jeannie, Julie, Elizabeth, and Alissa. You're my gifts from God to make this study stronger than I could have accomplished on my own.

To Erin Caruso, brainstorming and fine-tuning Bible studies with you is one of my favorite parts of writing. Thank you for your passion to help me enable readers grow in their knowledge and love of our triune God through His holy Word.

To my faithful prayer group and the leadership at Grace Bible Church, your prayers surround me and propel me forward. Your friendships fill me with courage, hope, and joy. The outstanding teaching equips me and motivates me to share what I'm learning with the world. Thank you!

To my beloved husband Larry. No one loves, encourages, or supports me more or greater than you. I'm forever thankful to God for bringing us together. You're my hero.

To Larry's and my amazing family, you're why I lock myself up in my studio to write when I'd rather be with you in person. Confusing, right? But I know that nothing will benefit your life more than knowing God and His Word. Nothing will give you more joy or hold you stronger than knowing and believing Christ and His Word. So I hide away for a while to write and pray that my written words will encourage you to seek the Lord with your whole heart through His Word. I love you all so much, Bobby, Kaitlyn, Samuel, Ophelia, Brittany, Carolyn, Melissa, Hannahbrooke, Rob, Kathy, Katelyn, Morgan, Kristy, Gus, Elliot, Kimbi, Karl, Mema, Laura, Andrew, Ken, Karen, Jake, and Candace.

Spread the Word by Doing One Thing.

- Give a copy of this book as a gift.
- Share the QR code link via your social media.
- Write a review of this book on your blog, favorite bookseller's website, or at ourdailybreadpublishing.org.
- Recommend this book to your church, small group, or book club.

Connect with us. [f] [⊙]

Our Daily Bread Publishing
PO Box 3566, Grand Rapids, MI 49501, USA
Email: books@odbm.org

Also Available

An 8-Week Transformational Bible Study of
HABAKKUK

embracing joy

JEAN WILUND

Love God. Love Others.
with Our Daily Bread.

Your gift changes lives.

Connect with us.

Our Daily Bread Publishing
PO Box 3566, Grand Rapids, MI 49501, USA
Email: books@odbm.org